Number 140
Winter 2013

New Directions for Evaluation

Paul R. Brandon
Editor-in-Chief

Data Visualization, Part 2

Tarek Azzam
Stephanie Evergreen
Editors

DATA VISUALIZATION, PART 2
Tarek Azzam, Stephanie Evergreen (eds.)
New Directions for Evaluation, no. 140
Paul R. Brandon, Editor-in-Chief

Microfilm copies of issues and articles are available in 16mm and 35mm, as well as microfiche in 105mm, through University Microfilms Inc., 300 North Zeeb Road, Ann Arbor, MI 48106-1346.

New Directions for Evaluation is indexed in Education Research Complete (EBSCO Publishing), ERIC: Education Resources Information Center (CSC), Higher Education Abstracts (Claremont Graduate University), SCOPUS (Elsevier), Social Services Abstracts (ProQuest), Sociological Abstracts (ProQuest), and Worldwide Political Science Abstracts (ProQuest).

NEW DIRECTIONS FOR EVALUATION (ISSN 1097-6736, electronic ISSN 1534-875X) is part of The Jossey-Bass Education Series and is published quarterly by Wiley Subscription Services, Inc., A Wiley Company, at Jossey-Bass, One Montgomery Street, Suite 1200, San Francisco, CA 94104-4594.

SUBSCRIPTIONS for individuals cost $89 for U.S./Canada/Mexico; $113 international. For institutions, $334 U.S.; $374 Canada/Mexico; $408 international. Electronic only: $89 for individuals all regions; $334 for institutions all regions. Print and electronic: $98 for individuals in the U.S., Canada, and Mexico; $122 for individuals for the rest of the world; $387 for institutions in the U.S.; $427 for institutions in Canada and Mexico; $461 for institutions for the rest of the world.

EDITORIAL CORRESPONDENCE should be addressed to the Editor-in-Chief, Paul R. Brandon, University of Hawai'i at Mānoa, 1776 University Avenue, Castle Memorial Hall Rm 118, Honolulu, HI 96822-2463.

www.josseybass.com

Editorial Policy and Procedures

New Directions for Evaluation, a quarterly sourcebook, is an official publication of the American Evaluation Association. The journal publishes works on all aspects of evaluation, with an emphasis on presenting timely and thoughtful reflections on leading-edge issues of evaluation theory, practice, methods, the profession, and the organizational, cultural, and societal context within which evaluation occurs. Each issue of the journal is devoted to a single topic, with contributions solicited, organized, reviewed, and edited by one or more guest editors.

The editor-in-chief is seeking proposals for journal issues from around the globe about topics new to the journal (although topics discussed in the past can be revisited). A diversity of perspectives and creative bridges between evaluation and other disciplines, as well as chapters reporting original empirical research on evaluation, are encouraged. A wide range of topics and substantive domains is appropriate for publication, including evaluative endeavors other than program evaluation; however, the proposed topic must be of interest to a broad evaluation audience. For examples of the types of topics that have been successfully proposed, go to http://www.josseybass.com/WileyCDA/Section/id-155510.html.

Journal issues may take any of several forms. Typically they are presented as a series of related chapters, but they might also be presented as a debate; an account, with critique and commentary, of an exemplary evaluation; a feature-length article followed by brief critical commentaries; or perhaps another form proposed by guest editors.

Submitted proposals must follow the format found via the Association's website at http://www.eval.org/Publications/NDE.asp. Proposals are sent to members of the journal's Editorial Advisory Board and to relevant substantive experts for single-blind peer review. The process may result in acceptance, a recommendation to revise and resubmit, or rejection. The journal does not consider or publish unsolicited single manuscripts.

Before submitting proposals, all parties are asked to contact the editor-in-chief, who is committed to working constructively with potential guest editors to help them develop acceptable proposals. For additional information about the journal, see the "Statement of the Editor-in-Chief" in the Spring 2013 issue (No. 137).

Paul R. Brandon, Editor-in-Chief
University of Hawai'i at Mānoa
College of Education
1776 University Avenue
Castle Memorial Hall, Rm. 118
Honolulu, HI 96822–2463
e-mail: nde@eval.org

Contents

Editor-in-Chief's Comment

With the guest editors, I am proud to present the second of two *New Directions for Evaluation* (NDE) issues on the topic of data visualization. The substantial number of figures and tables made it impossible to present all the chapters on the topic in a single journal issue. The guest editors and chapter authors introduced readers to the topic in the four chapters of NDE No. 139 (Fall 2013); the present second part includes an additional four chapters with numerous tables and figures demonstrating how evaluation results and statistics can be displayed effectively and attractively.

Readers should note that the tables and figures shown in the two NDE issues are available (many in color) at www.ndedataviz.com

Paul R. Brandon, PhD
Professor of Education
Curriculum Research & Development Group
College of Education
University of Hawai'i at Mānoa
Honolulu

New Directions for Evaluation, no. 140, Winter 2013 © Wiley Periodicals, Inc., and the American Evaluation Association. Published online in Wiley Online Library (wileyonlinelibrary.com) • DOI: 10.1002/ev.20069

Editors' Notes

The current crop of technological innovations has made it easier for evaluators to visualize data and information, but has also opened a Pandora's box for further frustrations, as common visualization errors continue. The methods of display have also vastly increased in the past few years, as software capacity develops and online tools grow in popularity. Given the spread and the growing expectations for visualizations among stakeholders, it is ever more important that evaluators remain current on the opportunities and challenges that data visualization offers. This issue of *New Directions for Evaluation*, the second of two parts, aims to introduce evaluators to different qualitative and quantitative applications that can be used in evaluation practice. The issue also offers concrete suggestions for improving data visualization design and helps the reader identify and correct common visualization errors that can often lead to communication failures. Our goal is to introduce the reader to some practical and fundamental ideas and concepts in data visualization. Part 1 (*New Directions for Evaluation*, 139) introduced readers to the tools and status of data visualization, with general overviews of how it is used on both quantitative and qualitative data. Both Parts 1 and 2 are intended as references and as sources for guidance and ideas for evaluators who are interested in, designing, and struggling with data visualizations.

The beginning of each chapter contains icons (designed by Chris Metzner) that indicate the applicability of the chapter to the four stages of the evaluation life cycle (Alkin, 2010). These stages include (1) understanding the program, stakeholders, and context; (2) collecting data and information; (3) analyzing data; and (4) communicating findings (see Figure 1). These icons provide a quick reference of each chapter's content and its relationship to evaluation practice.

Figure 1. Title Icons

Understanding

Collecting

Analyzing

Communicating

New Directions for Evaluation, no. 140, Winter 2013 © Wiley Periodicals, Inc., and the American Evaluation Association. Published online in Wiley Online Library (wileyonlinelibrary.com) • DOI: 10.1002/ev.20070

Part 2 Chapter Descriptions

Chapter 5 offers general guidelines and best practices for good data visualization, which focus on addressing common errors and using techniques to help a viewer understand and interpret the data. Chapter 6 introduces readers to data dashboards, discusses their history and uses for strategic decision making, and outlines a step-by-step process for creating an effective data dashboard. In Chapter 7, readers are introduced to the graphic recording process, a visualization method that involves audiences during the evaluation process and helps stakeholders share their knowledge and make sense of relevant data. Chapter 8 provides readers with examples of how maps and geographic information systems (GIS) can be used during the evaluation process to assess needs, track implementation, and examine program outcomes. In all cases, the figures in each chapter have been printed in black and white; color versions can be found at ndedataviz.com

Reference

Alkin, M. C. (2010). *Evaluation essentials: From A to Z.* New York, NY: Guilford Press.

Tarek Azzam
Stephanie Evergreen
Editors

TAREK AZZAM *is an assistant professor at Claremont Graduate University and associate director of the Claremont Evaluation Center.*

STEPHANIE EVERGREEN *is an evaluator who runs Evergreen Data, a data presentation consulting firm.*

NEW DIRECTIONS FOR EVALUATION • DOI: 10.1002/ev

Evergreen, S., & Metzner, C. (2013). Design principles for data visualization in evaluation. In T. Azzam & S. Evergreen (Eds.), *Data visualization, part 2. New Directions for Evaluation, 140,* 5–20.

5

Design Principles for Data Visualization in Evaluation

Stephanie Evergreen, Chris Metzner

Abstract

Data visualization is often used in two main ways—as a tool to aid analysis or as a tool for communication. In the context of this issue, in this chapter we are focusing on the latter. At its most essential, the communication goal of data visualization is to grab audience attention and help them engage with the data such that the resulting product is increased understanding, regardless of the software platform or programming ability of the author. © Wiley Periodicals, Inc., and the American Evaluation Association.

I n her influential article summarizing the state of evaluation use, Weiss (1998) ends with this thought:

> The evaluator has to seek many routes to communication—through conferences, workshops, professional media, mass media, think tanks, clearinghouses, interest groups, policy networks—whatever it takes to get important findings into circulation. And then we have to keep our fingers crossed that audiences pay attention. (p. 32)

Note: The figures presented in this chapter can be viewed in color by accessing www .NDEdataviz.com and selecting Chapter 5.

NEW DIRECTIONS FOR EVALUATION, no. 140, Winter 2013 © Wiley Periodicals, Inc., and the American Evaluation Association. Published online in Wiley Online Library (wileyonlinelibrary.com) • DOI: 10.1002/ev.20071

This chapter will pick up where Weiss left off by investigating the role of communication in supporting the attention of evaluation audiences. Visualization-supported evaluation reporting is an educational act and, as such, should be communicated with the use of principles that support cognition. Research from related fields suggests practices evaluators could do (and may be doing) to increase the chances that audiences will want to engage with their reporting. One study found a very high correlation of .91 between perceived beauty of a display and its usefulness (Tractinsky, 1997). Evaluators can do much more than cross their fingers and hope their data will be read and used.

The main difference between effective and ineffective data displays is their ability to communicate the evaluator's key message in a clear and straightforward way such that it does not overload a viewer's working memory capacity. This chapter will discuss methods, borrowed from graphic design and tested in survey research and user interface programming, that evaluators can use to highlight data effectively. Graphic designers have been using the models of cognition to make better displays—whether computer (Johnson, 2010) or paper (Ware, 2012)—and here we borrow heavily from their research and that of sister fields to offer general guidelines for creating data visualization (Evergreen, 2011a; Few, 2009). Models of cognition are the theories about how the brain intakes, interprets, and retains information. The chapter will focus on two main concepts that work from models of cognition to support meaningful data visualizations—simplification and emphasis.

Simplification

Graphic designers support comprehension by simplifying visualizations to the extent possible (Few, 2008, 2009; Jamet, Garota, & Quaireau, 2008; Malamed, 2009; Reynolds, 2009; Samara, 2007; Stenberg, 2006). Simplification strategies include discouraging three-dimensional displays, removing extraneous gridlines and decimals, and avoiding color gradation, all of which Tufte (2001) refers to as "visual noise" (p. 105) and "non-data ink" (p. 96), terms he coined to refer to anything that does not directly aid the understanding of the data in the display. Research in this area has shown that readers will abandon overly complex graphs, rather than muddle through their interpretation to make meaning (Chen & Yu, 2000; Shah, Mayer, & Hegarty, 1999).

Compare these data visualizations in Figures 5.1 and 5.2, both made in Excel. Figure 5.1 is the product of Excel's automatic graph generation. It carries a great deal of visual noise, including unnecessary tick marks, gridlines, color changes, and two decimal places. Figure 5.2 has been simplified, still in Excel, so that what remains is primarily the ink that supports the comprehension of the data. In this example, the evaluator is using a different color to bring attention to the water treatment needs of an infrastructure project.

Figure 5.1. Default Settings Can Create Too Much "Visual Noise"

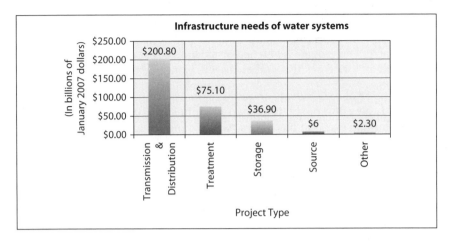

Figure 5.2. Simplification Keeps the Focus on the Data

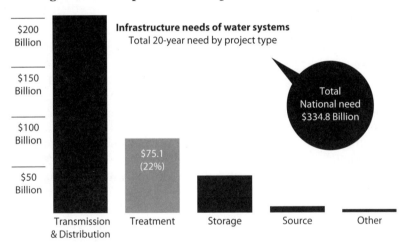

Excel is a powerful tool for data visualization, but it sometimes gives the user many unhelpful options that quickly complicate a data display. Sometimes we have to remove data display elements, particularly those in Excel's default options, to create a more useful graph. For example, viewer comprehension of data visualization can benefit from gridlines or data point labels, but not both. If exact values are important to communicate, use data labels (or consider a table). If the communication goal is to display overall trends and estimated values, use faint gridlines. Working memory can only hold roughly four chunks or bits of information (e.g., numbers, tasks, etc.) at one time (Cowan, 2000; Xu & Chun, 2006). This places limits on the cognitive load an audience member can bear. Thus, graph designers may need to strip away built-in features to reduce the number of operating elements in the display.

Legend

The presence of a visualization along with associated text brings greater recall and retention of the information (Johnson, 2010; Stenberg, 2006). Because human eyesight has only a narrow range of focus, graphics should be placed very near their associated text (Malamed, 2009; Ware, 2012). The common practice of placing graphs in an appendix or separated by pages from their corresponding text means that some information will be lost in the extended time a reader must take to flip back and forth to bring the text and the graphic together into a comprehensive whole. Similarly, if a legend is required in the visualization, it should be so near the corresponding data points that no eye movements are needed to relate the two.

Preferably, remove the legend altogether to simplify the back-and-forth needed to match up the entry to its related data points. Direct labeling reduces the viewer's cognitive load and allows for more efficient mental processing.

Data

We also creep toward claustrophobic graphs when we overload the display (on the next page—we know) with too much text. We've been trained as evaluators to report not just the survey responses, for example, but also the sample size. Usually, our intention is to be transparent and communicate to the viewer that, say, a different number of respondents replied to each survey question. It can lead to graphs that look like that in Figure 5.3.

Although there are circumstances where wildly different sample sizes are cause for alarm, most of the time, it is of secondary importance. Their inclusion in the data display complicates the graph and strains working memory likely more than any benefit they might provide. The few readers who will care very much about the sample size should still be able to access that information, such as in a hover popout box or in a table in an appendix, where supporting information belongs.

Similarly, segmenting complicated information into smaller chunks helps the reader assimilate the information into an existing schema. To reduce the risk of overload, the designer often predigests some of the information, like the way a graph represents some mental processing that would have had to take place in the viewer's brain if she was simply reading the information as gray narrative text. The designer "pre-chunks," essentially allowing more information into working memory than would otherwise be possible. One way this could occur is through using small multiples, which declutter the visual display, an example of which is shown in Figure 5.4.

NEW DIRECTIONS FOR EVALUATION • DOI: 10.1002/ev

Figure 5.3. Too Much Detail in Data Labels Is Distracting

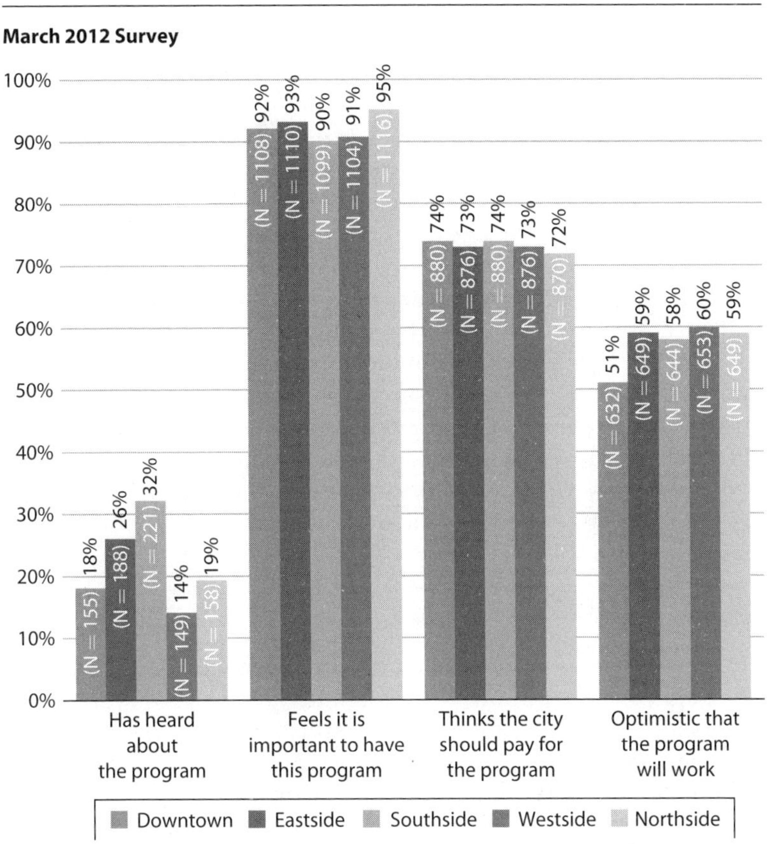

March 2012 Survey

Designers might also keep things simple through the use of signs or symbols, even in data displays. Symbols are instantly recognizable and quickly communicate your message with less interpretation and cognitive activity on the part of the viewer (Tappenden, Jefford, & Farris, 2004). Icons or symbols can be used as data labels or to otherwise organize data in a visualization.

Color

For color to be used well, secondary information or data points should be simplified to a shade of gray so that chosen elements can appropriately stand out when selected emphasis colors are applied. Graph background colors should generally be white or have very subdued colors (Tufte, 1990; Ware, 2008; Wheildon, 2005), without any sort of pattern or color gradation (Williams, 2000). Graph text should be dark gray or black (Samara,

Figure 5.4. Small Multiples Show Data on the Same Variables for Multiple Locations, Using Simpler Displays

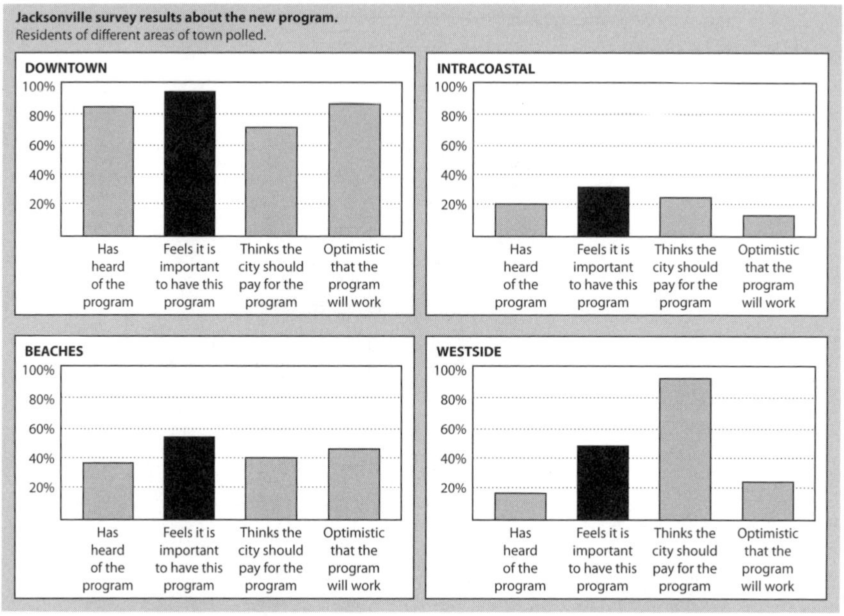

Jacksonville survey results about the new program.
Residents of different areas of town polled.

2007; Ware, 2008; Wheildon, 2005) for maximum contrast with the background, and thus, higher legibility. Just as in paintings, pure hues and brighter colors tend to create the mood, but grays and neutrals are the foundation that allows the colors to pop. Grays and neutrals are gentle on the eye and naturally complement any color nearby (Few, 2008; Quiller, 1999; Tufte, 2001).

The Excel default color scheme can actually impede comprehension because the colors are assigned indiscriminately; readers expect that a change in color indicates a change in meaning and they will spend time and effort trying to understand the meaning shift when the choice of color usually holds no meaning at all (Few, 2008; Jamet et al., 2008; Malamed, 2009; Samara, 2007; Tufte, 1997; Ware, 2008). Moreover, as you can see in the example that we made with the Excel default color scheme, those colors do not have much integrity when reproduced in black-and-white (see Figure 5.5).

Stripping away the unnecessary and deemphasizing the supporting information simplifies the data display so that the more extraneous does not distract or avert the viewer's attention. A simpler display also lays the groundwork for adding in selected emphasis to draw the viewer's attention to areas of higher importance.

NEW DIRECTIONS FOR EVALUATION • DOI: 10.1002/ev

Figure 5.5. Imagine This Column Graph in the Excel Default Colors of (Left to Right) Blue, Red, Green, and Purple

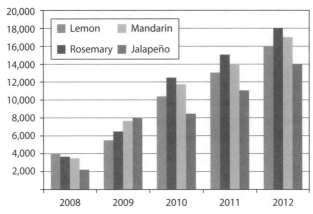

Importing infusion scents
Quantities rise as programs help increase production

Emphasis

Once a data visualization has been simplified to its most communicative parts, specific points in the visualization can be emphasized to aid the viewer in interpretation. Empirical studies have shown that using attention-guiding design elements, like orientation and contrast, significantly increase interpretation accuracy and long-term recall of information (Faraday & Sutcliffe, 1997; Joshi & Rheingans, 2008). Increasing size, for example, is one way to draw attention to the most important elements of the data display (or to the display itself), as is increasing the white space around the display (Williams, 2000). This section will discuss and display techniques to emphasize data. Essentially, most emphasis techniques come down to creating contrast between elements of a data display. Emphasis and contrast will be detailed in terms of use of color, weight, motion, text, and arrows.

Color

Color, as an area of study, has become more prominent than other aspects of design because technology has made working with color more accessible in recent years. Color is one of the quickest elements to capture attention. For normally sighted individuals, it has a long history of being able to catch the human eye. The danger of the color red in the animal kingdom, for example, is well-known. Contemporary graphic designers use color in a similar way—to draw attention to selective elements of interest (Reynolds, 2009; Samara, 2007; Tufte, 1990; Wheildon, 2005). Color cues provide

NEW DIRECTIONS FOR EVALUATION • DOI: 10.1002/ev

Figure 5.6. The Top Bar and Its Label Are Set in a Darker Color to Stand Out Against the Other Data

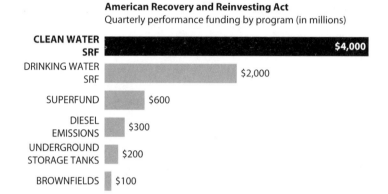

information that makes for improved assessment and decision making (Campbell & Maglio, 1999).

As you may have noticed, we will address the use of color through a printed medium that is restricted to showing black-and-white images. Such a scenario is not all that different from those we experience as evaluators working with budget-conscious clients who operate with black-and-white printers. The full-color versions of these displays are also available online.[1]

Color, then, should be judiciously applied when the designer is attempting to bring attention to a specific data point or intentionally build a color-coding scheme. For categorical data graphed in a bar chart, research suggests the best option would be choosing the same color for all bars, except for the bar that needs the most attention, such as those falling below the cut score or those representing your particular program (see Figure 5.6).

For ordinal and ratio data, shades of one color can adequately communicate the related nature of the data. But even here, if attention needs to be brought to a single line, for example, the others can be deemphasized by shifting their colors to a neutral gray and letting the line in question remain in its full, emphasized, color (see Figure 5.7).

However, colors may be problematic if they are too bright and distract the reader from the rest of the text (Wheildon, 2005), or if they do not sufficiently contrast with the background to be legible (Few, 2008; Malamed, 2009; Reynolds, 2009; Samara, 2007; Ware, 2008). Ultimately, the precise color combinations matter less than their contrast, as shown below (see Figures 5.8 and 5.9).

Color choice relies upon the mindfulness of the designer, but some colors have strong cultural connotations that should be considered when making design choices (Clarke & Costall, 2008; Malamed, 2009). Yellow is a good example of a popular color choice when a designer needs to call attention to a specific area. Yellow expresses bright, cheerful, warming, and

Figure 5.7. The Reference Line is Deemphasized With a Light Gray, and the More Important Line Is a Bold Green

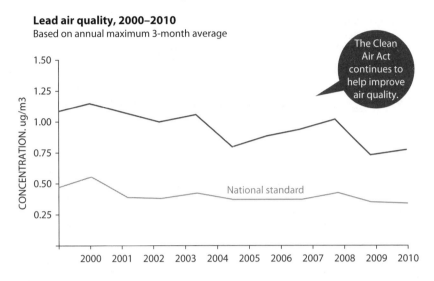

Figure 5.8. Low Contrast With a Color Background Makes the Data Difficult to See

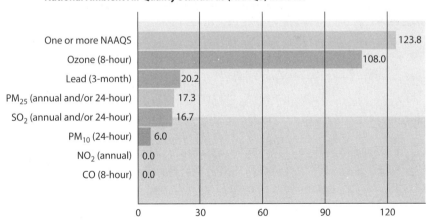

stimulating feelings, but if overused, it can evoke the opposite. Moses (2007, p. 37) writes, "studies show that babies cry more in yellow rooms. In Western culture, yellow has also traditionally symbolized cowardice." Moreover, it would not contrast well with the recommended light-colored chart background.

Figure 5.9. A White Background With Bold Colored Bars Keeps the Contrast High

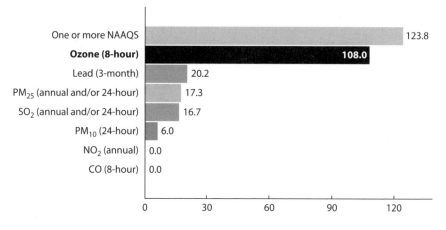

Number of people (in millions) living in counties with air quality concentrations above the level of the primary (health-based) National Ambient Air Quality Standards (NAAQS) in 2010.

Additionally, certain color combinations, such as red–green or blue–yellow, cause difficulty for people with color blindness and should generally be avoided unless the contrast between the pair is significant enough to maintain a distinction. Software programs like Vischeck (http://www.vischeck.com/) and Color Oracle (http://colororacle.org/) can be superimposed over a visualization to show what it would look like to people with color-blindness.

Weight

Just as color contrast can emphasize key parts of a data display, so can visual weight. Things that are similar in appearance are interpreted as being close in meaning, thus creating any sort of visual difference communicates a change in meaning (Tourangeau, Couper, & Conrad, 2004). Heavier weights are interpreted as more important, more attention grabbing, than lighter weights. In terms of a line graph, weight can be modified by increasing the width of a particular line. In a scatter plot, for example, adjust weight by varying the size (and color) of individual data points (see Figure 5.10).

Motion

As data displays are rendered online, the use of motion to emphasize key content has become increasingly popular. When in an online environment, users tend to expect interactivity and motion is a primary method for emphasizing user-selected data. Motion has been shown to attract attention even when a viewer is already engaged with the screen (Hillstrom & Yantis, 1994).

Figure 5.10. The Data Point for the Country Under Investigation Can Be Emphasized by Increasing Its Width or Size

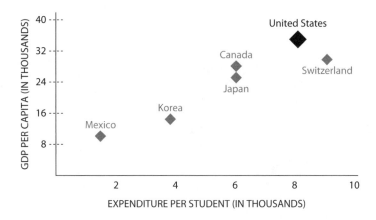

Annual expenditures on public and private institutions
Per student as a percentage of country's GDP: 2000

When users interact with the online version of the Paint Stewardship Model different parts of the display become activated (see Figures 5.11 and 5.12). Hovering over the numerals, for example, opens a pop-up dialogue box with more details. Other parts of the display reveal short videos and other interactive features that come to the viewer's foreground through a sweeping pop-up motion.

Text and Arrows

Though we have taken pains to remove unnecessary text and decorative elements from a data visualization, intentionally and carefully bringing some back in can support reader interpretation.

Perhaps the most obvious attention-guiding element is the universal arrow. We know that the arrow has been shown to increase responses to key items on survey questionnaires (Christian & Dillman, 2004). The presence of arrows causes shifts in attention (Faraday & Sutcliffe, 1997). Although perhaps not an appropriate addition to the graph itself, an arrow could be overlaid on a data visualization to focus attention on one particular area. It could then be removed and placed elsewhere to guide a viewer around a display.

In our practical experience, graphs placed in technical reports often need to stand on their own, in that the busy stakeholder may not have the time to read the surrounding narrative explanation. Thus, a better use of the graph's title space can help interpret the data for the viewer. Rather than a generic or obtuse title, the graph title can be used to convey the "so what" about the display. Additionally, a descriptive subtitle can extend the explanation to report the

Figure 5.11. The Basic Web-Based Paint Stewardship Model Is Shown

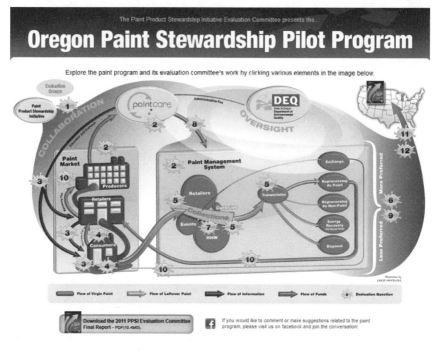

Figure 5.12. Interaction Causes Content to Move to the Foreground for Closer Inspection

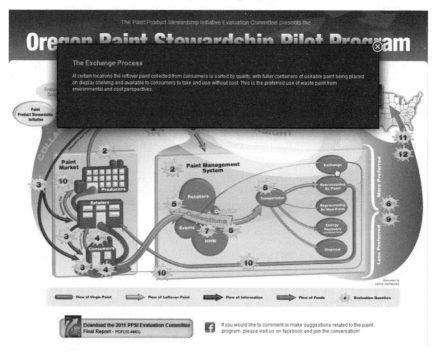

Figure 5.13. Additional Text Can Be Added to a Graph to Emphasize Key Findings or Important Details

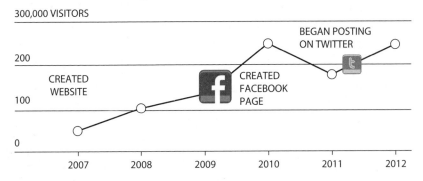

Using social media webites to attract customers
Visits increased after launching social media, then fell a bit with the national trend.

correlation, identify which bar colors need staff attention, or how the data benchmark against the program's peers, just to name a few examples.

Text can also be added back into the graph to provide annotation. For example, when critical points in time need to be shown on a time-series display, an evaluator can insert a textbox over the graph to annotate the additional details needed to interpret the visualization and make the impact obvious. Annotations can be used to call out certain data points and provide an extra level of detail that is useful when a viewer must digest a graph on his or her own. The graph in Figure 5.13 shows the use of both a descriptive subtitle and annotation along the data line.

Even with the emphasis techniques we've listed here and the others you may have thought of while reading, we impress upon the need to remain judicious in the application of emphasis. The simultaneous use of too many emphasis techniques drains their power and can even damage the credibility of the presenter or author (Thota, Song, & Larsen, 2010). Overemphasis ultimately reproduces the cluttered look and feel we began with when discussing simplification (see Figure 5.3). Emphasis can only do its job if we are selective in our application. Thus, the balance between simplification and emphasis is always delicate and tense.

Implications for Evaluation Practice

Why should any of this matter to evaluators? Like graphic designers, we are in the business of communication. Thus, the way we package our words and our data reflects on audience perception—both in terms of their views of our credibility and their ability to cognate our message accurately. Yet in Evergreen's (2011b) study on the extent of graphic design use in evaluation reporting, evaluation practitioners rated graphics—including graphs and charts, the basics of data visualization—as the least used area in the reports they reviewed. Graphics were poorly used or even absent altogether. Recently, the International Development Research Centre's (IDRC) Evaluation Unit undertook a similar study (Strecker, 2012) of its own reporting products and found that about half contained data visualizations. Of those, many were overreliant on the default graph settings, resulting in cloudy visualizations that lacked a clear message. The study concluded that many evaluation report authors at IDRC were enthusiastic about designing better graphs but did not yet know the best practices to apply. Kosslyn et al.'s (2012) study, which included data displays as part of slideshows, surfaced multiple widespread violations of cognitive communication principles, where overcomplication was also among the top mistakes.

Essentially, creating difference, creating something out of the ordinary, calls attention (Hillstrom & Yantis, 1994; Treisman, 1988). Thoughtful and strategic use of these graphic design principles in our data visualization attract the reader to a visualization, aid the reader in interpreting the data, and support the reader's attempts to comprehend the evaluation findings. Data visualizations ranked as more beautiful were abandoned less frequently and supported more accurate responses. In one study, subjects were also willing to spend more time digesting and interpreting the data visualizations that were better designed (Cawthon & Moere, 2007). We have long known that as graph complexity increases, recall of the information displayed decreases (Lusk & Kersnick, 1979). So although attractiveness is a splendid side effect, we engage in the intentional design of data visualizations in order to make our data more understandable.

What we are talking about here is no less than the very understanding of the work we do as evaluators. Well-designed visuals are particularly effective at enhancing recall and retention of information in our audiences. The effort we put into making data visualizations more interpretable pays off in more efficient engagement with the products of our evaluation endeavors. Thus, including the process of simplification and emphasis in our evaluation practice is an investment in and commitment to the learning needs of our primary intended users.

The chapters in this issue have highlighted specific methods of visualization that evaluators can employ to increase accessibility to their data. This chapter holds the position that if evaluators use the research-based guidelines illustrated here when employing the visualization methods described in the rest of the issue, our data will be better understood.

Endnote

1. ndedataviz.com

References

Campbell, C. S., & Maglio, P. P. (1999). Facilitating navigation in information spaces: Road-signs on the World Wide Web. *International Journal of Human–Computer Studies, 50,* 309–327.

Cawthon, N., & Moere, A. V. (2007, July). The effect of aesthetic on the usability of data visualization. In E. Banissi et al. (Eds.), *Information Visualization, 2007. IV '07. 11th International Conference,* Zurich, Switzerland.

Chen, C., & Yu, Y. (2000). Empirical studies of information visualization: A meta-analysis. *International Journal of Human–Computer Studies, 53*(5), 851–866.

Christian, L. M., & Dillman, D. A. (2004). The influence of graphical and symbolic language manipulations on responses to self-administered questions. *Public Opinion Quarterly, 68*(1), 57–80.

Clarke, T., & Costall, A. (2008). The emotional connotations of color: A qualitative investigation. *Color Research and Application, 33*(5), 406–410.

Cowan, N. (2000). The magical number 4 in short-term memory: A reconsideration of mental storage capacity. *Behavioral and Brain Sciences, 24,* 87–185.

Evergreen, S. D. H. (2011a). Eval + comm. *New Directions for Evaluation, 131,* 41–46.

Evergreen, S. D. H. (2011b). *Death by boredom: The role of visual processing theory in written evaluation communication* (Unpublished doctoral dissertation). Western Michigan University, Kalamazoo, MI.

Faraday, P., & Sutcliffe, A. (1997). Designing effective multimedia presentations. *CHI'97: Proceedings of the ACM SIGCHI Conference on Human Factors in Computing Systems* (pp. 272–278). New York, NY: ACM.

Few, S. (2008, February). Practical rules for using color in charts. *Visual Business Intelligence Newsletter.* Retrieved from http://www.perceptualedge.com/articles/visual_business_intelligence/rules_for_using_color.pdf

Few, S. (2009). *Now you see it: Simple visualization techniques for quantitative analysis.* Oakland, CA: Analytics Press.

Hillstrom, A. P., & Yantis, S. (1994). Visual motion and attentional capture. *Perception & Psychophysics, 55*(4), 399–411.

Jamet, E., Garota, M., & Quaireau, C. (2008). Attention guiding in multimedia learning. *Learning and Instruction, 18,* 135–145.

Johnson, J. (2010). *Designing with the mind in mind: Simple guide to understanding user interface design rules.* Burlington, MA: Morgan Kaufman.

Joshi, A., & Rheingans, P. (2008). Evaluation of illustration-inspired techniques for time-varying data visualization. In A. Vilanova, A. Telea, G. Scheuermann, & T. Moller (Eds.). *Eurographics/IEEE-VGTC Symposium on Visualization, 27*(3), 999–1006.

Kosslyn, S. M., Kievit, R. A., Russell, A. G., & Shephard, J. M. (2012). PowerPoint presentation flaws and failures: A psychological analysis. *Frontiers in Psychology, 3,* 1–22.

Lusk, E. J., & Kersnick, M. (1979). The effect of cognitive style and report format on task performance: The misdesign consequences. *Management Science, 25*(8), 787–798.

Malamed, C. (2009). *Visual language for designers: Principles for creating graphics that people understand.* Beverly, MA: Rockport.

Moses, M. (2007). *Understanding color: Creative techniques in watercolor.* New York, NY: Sterling.

Quiller, S. (1999). *Painter's guide to color.* New York, NY: Watson-Guptill.

Reynolds, G. (2009). *Presentation zen design: Simple design principles and techniques to enhance your presentations.* Berkeley, CA: New Riders Press.

Samara, T. (2007). *Design elements: A graphic style manual.* Beverly, MA: Rockport Press.

Shah, P., Mayer, R. E., & Hegarty, M. (1999). Graphs as aids to knowledge construction:

Signaling techniques for guiding the process of graph comprehension. *Journal of Educational Psychology, 91*(4), 690–702.

Stenberg, G. (2006). Conceptual and perceptual factors in the picture superiority effect. *European Journal of Cognitive Psychology, 18*, 813–847.

Strecker, J. (2012). Evaluating IDRC results: Communicating research for influence, data visualization in review: Summary. Ottawa, Canada: International Development Research Centre. Retrieved from http://www.idrc.ca/EN/Documents/Summary-Report-English-Final-7-May-2012.pdf

Tappenden, C., Jefford, L., & Farris, S. (2004). *Foundation course graphic design.* London, England: Cassell Illustrated.

Thota, S. C., Song, J. H., & Larsen, V. (2010). Do animated banner ads hurt websites? The moderating roles of website loyalty and need for cognition. *Academy of Marketing Studies Journal, 14*(1), 91–116.

Tourangeau, R., Couper, M. P., & Conrad, F. G. (2004). Spacing, position, and order: Interpretive heuristics for visual features of survey questions. *Public Opinion Quarterly, 68*(1), 368–393.

Tractinsky, N. (1997). Aesthetics and apparent usability: Empirically assessing cultural and methodological issues. In CHI'97: *Proceedings of the ACM SIGCHI Conference on Human Factors in Computing Systems* (pp. 115–122). Retrieved from http://old.sigchi.org/chi97/proceedings/paper/nt.htm

Treisman, A. (1988). Features and objects: The fourteenth Bartlett memorial lecture. The *Quarterly Journal of Experimental Psychology, 40A*(2), 201–237.

Tufte, E. R. (1990). *Envisioning information.* Cheshire, CT: Graphics Press.

Tufte, E. R. (1997). *Visual explanations: Images and quantities, evidence and narrative.* Cheshire, CT: Graphics Press.

Tufte, E. R. (2001). *The visual display of quantitative information* (2nd ed.). Cheshire, CT: Graphics Press.

Ware, C. (2008). *Visual thinking for design.* Waltham, MA: Morgan Kaufmann.

Ware, C. (2012). *Information visualization: Perception for design* (3rd ed.). Waltham, MA: Morgan Kaufmann.

Weiss, C. (1998). Have we learned anything new about the use of evaluation? *American Journal of Evaluation, 19*(1), 21–33.

Wheildon, C. (2005). *Type and layout: Are you communicating or just making pretty shapes?* Mentone, Australia: The Worsley Press.

Williams, T. R. (2000). Guidelines for designing and evaluating the display of information on the web. *Technical Communication, 47*(3), 383–396.

Xu, Y., & Chun, M. M. (2006). Dissociable neural mechanisms supporting visual short-term memory for objects. *Nature, 440*, 91–95.

STEPHANIE EVERGREEN *is an evaluator who runs Evergreen Data, a data presentation consulting firm.*

CHRIS METZNER *is a freelance graphic designer, creating print and web-related projects to help his clients achieve their unique advertising needs and marketing goals.*

Smith, V. S. (2013). Data dashboard as evaluation and research communication tool. In
T. Azzam & S. Evergreen (Eds.), *Data visualization, part 2. New Directions for Evaluation,*
140, 21–45.

6

Data Dashboard as Evaluation and Research Communication Tool

Veronica S. Smith

Abstract

Data dashboards are visual displays that feature the most important informa-
tion needed to achieve specific goals captured on a single screen. Effective dash-
boards should be designed as monitoring tools that are understood at a glance.
Dashboards are useful tools because they can leverage visual perception to com-
municate dense amounts of data clearly and concisely. They are typically used in
the communication phase of evaluation; however, in the case of analytical dash-
boards, they may also be used in the analysis phase. Strategic, analytical, and
operational dashboards are different dashboard types used to meet different
communication needs. This chapter highlights keys to realizing the potential of
data dashboards by describing appropriate use, effective practices for designing
and creating these tools, how to evaluate dashboards, and software that can be
used to create dashboards. © Wiley Periodicals, Inc., and the American Evaluation Association.

Note: The figures presented in this chapter can be viewed in color by accessing www
.NDEdataviz.com and selecting Chapter 6.

The working definition of a data dashboard comes from information design thought leader Stephen Few: A dashboard "is a visual display of the most important information needed to achieve one or more objectives consolidated on a single screen so it can be monitored and understood at a glance" (Few, 2006, p. 12). This chapter discusses both dashboards and dashboard reports. Although dashboards consolidate all measures on a single screen or page (Figure 6.1), a dashboard report typically will include multiple screens or pages with one or two measures reported per page/screen (Figure 6.2).

The dashboard as a communication tool was born out of the history of executive information systems (EISs) in the 1980s (Thierauf, 1991). The EIS never made it outside executive offices; only a few were used. EISs were designed to display a limited amount of high-level performance indicators that could be easily understood by those at the C suite level. The technological advances in the 1990s, including data warehousing, cheaper computer memory, increased processor speed, and demand for evidence-based decision making, set the stage for new interest in and capacity to manage using metrics. The 1990s also saw the emergence of the Kaplan and Norton (1996) balanced scorecard, which proposed an approach for telling the story of a business unit's strategy from more than a financial perspective by linking performance and outcome indicators.

In addition to the development of technology and thought leadership, the 2001 Enron scandal aftermath increased pressure on organizations to demonstrate their monitoring abilities. The push for increased accountability along with the economic downturn motivated Chief Information Officers to find tools that could help all managers more easily keep an eye on performance. This chain of events led to a marketplace with a wide selection of business intelligence (BI) tools from which to choose, including dashboard software (Few, 2006).

The use of BI in for-profit industries has subsequently influenced the adoption of dashboards in social sector/nonprofit organizations. Nonprofit governance has also received increased scrutiny by the media, regulatory agencies, and the public at large (Butler, 2007). Board and program leaders' ability to access critical outcome and performance information quickly is more important than ever. Furthermore, social sector/nonprofit organizations have experienced a rise in accountability demands from funders, including pressure to demonstrate compliance and evaluation of their work (Carman, 2007; Kopczynski & Pritchard, 2004). The Obama Administration's FY 2011 budget stated, "Government operates more effectively when it focuses on outcomes, when leaders set clear and measurable goals, and when agencies use measurement to reinforce priorities, motivate action, and illuminate a path to improvement" (U.S. Office of Management and Budget, 2010, p. 73). The Obama budget went on to praise the use of dashboards pioneered in state and local governments specifically as tools to monitor and take action that will improve performance (Kamensky, 2011). These statements capture

Figure 6.1. Dashboard Used to Inform a Board of Directors' Strategic Decision Making for a Nonprofit Organization That Provides Elementary Education Enrichment Programs

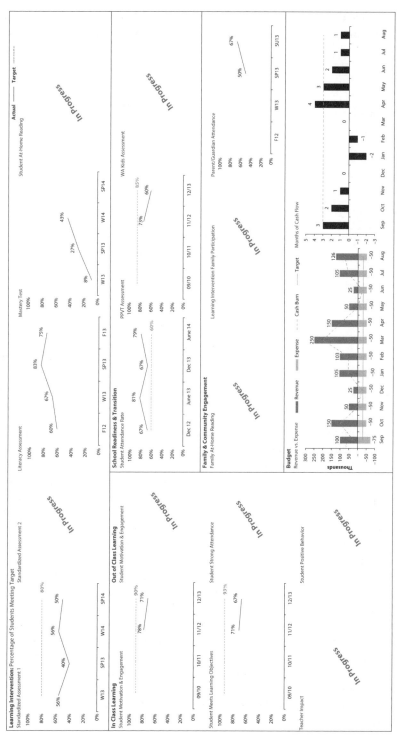

2012–13 Performance Measures

Figure 6.2. Part of a 24-Page Dashboard Report Used to Inform a Fictitious Energy Company's Performance Management, With Two to Three Measures Per Page

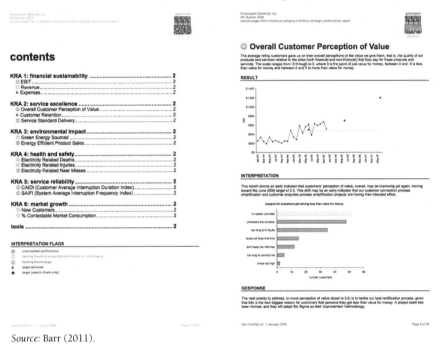

Source: Barr (2011).

the sentiment of many funders today. They want to know how programs and services will result in desired changes or outcomes.

Despite the increased scrutiny and demand for performance measurement, nonprofit managers are too often unable to respond adequately (Newcomer, 2004). We are now in the midst of a business intelligence industry obsession called *big data*, which refers to the increased volume of data available, speed of data creation, and variety of digital data sources that are available for analytics (McAfee & Brynjolfsson, 2012). These developments have helped the EIS seeds planted decades ago bloom. Nevertheless, more data faster is not what evaluators and their clients need; they need the means to filter the signal from the noise. This is where the data dashboard can help. However, effective dashboard design and application does not necessarily follow from dashboard software or templates being readily available. In fact, dashboards can degrade the signal and increase the noise, depending on the design, software, management, use, and context (Figure 6.3).

This chapter aims to provide a sound framework and guidelines for evaluators, researchers, and program staff to design, develop, maintain, and use a data dashboard as an effective communication tool for monitoring progress and performance against specific objectives.

NEW DIRECTIONS FOR EVALUATION • DOI: 10.1002/ev

Figure 6.3. A Dashboard Design That Gets in the Way of Effective Communication Instead of Enhancing It

When to Use Dashboards

Drivers and pilots use the gauges on dashboards to inform their decisions, and rely on those instruments to give them the most critical information at a glance in order to make timely decisions that will result in arriving at their desired destination. The movement of the needle signals to the driver or pilot that a change has occurred that needs to be taken into consideration. The image of the moving needle gets at the primary value of the dashboard for the evaluator's monitoring and reporting toolkit: the ability to better leverage stakeholders' most powerful sense—vision—to make evidence-based decisions.

As with any tool, it is important to understand when its use is appropriate. Dashboards primarily support quantitative measures of outputs and/or outcomes with some type of comparison. Dashboards are used to monitor critical information needed to accomplish an objective or set of objectives. Most of the information that does this best is quantitative (Few, 2006). However, not all information needed to accomplish goals can be expressed numerically. Simple lists are fairly common on dashboards, especially those that involve project or process management. For example, tasks that need to be completed, due dates, people responsible or who needs to be contacted, issues that need to be addressed, and top 10 performers are all types of qualitative data occasionally found on dashboards (see Figure 6.4).

Figure 6.4. Operational Dashboard Design Illustrating Use of Quantitative Data in Major Project Milestones, Five Top Projects, and Critical Events Sections

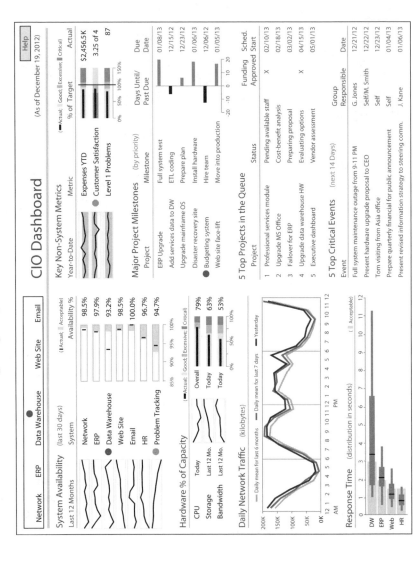

Source: Few (2013b).

Data dashboards are typically used for the following three purposes:

- **Strategic purposes.** The most common purpose of dashboards that support management is strategic. Strategic dashboards give a 30,000-foot view of the performance of a program or organization (Few, 2006). The refresh cycle for these dashboards is typically monthly or quarterly (Figure 6.5).
- **Analytical purposes.** Dashboards for analytical purposes are typically used by data analysts, policy makers, evaluators, and researchers. They should be interactive and allow the user to drill down into the details of the data (on the same or separate screens) and support exploration and examination (Figure 6.6). The refresh cycle for an analytical dashboard could be daily, weekly, monthly, quarterly, or yearly.
- **Operational purposes.** When monitoring operations, the aim is keep a finger on the pulse of activities and events that are in constant flux and may require attention and response at any given moment (see Figure 6.7). This type of dashboard is primarily for formative, quality assurance, or safety purposes. The refresh cycle for an operational dashboard is typically less than a minute. Display media in this case must grab user attention immediately if an operation falls outside given performance parameters.

Recently the data visualization firm Perceptual Edge sponsored a dashboard design competition that asked participants to design a student performance dashboard, intended for use by the teacher prior to each class session "to prevent or resolve problems and to help each student improve as much as possible" (Few, 2012a, paragraph 1). Few designed a dashboard, seen in Figure 6.7, pulling together the best features of the two winning designs. This example supports both analytical and operational functionality, illustrating that dashboards do not always fall into exactly one of the three categories previously outlined. The teacher could quickly determine that students Kim, Chandler, and Francis need some attention to get their math achievement back on track. This is an operational function. This dashboard is designed to have a drill-down function on assignments so the teacher could get more detail, providing a powerful analysis function. The teacher could also conduct exploratory and explanatory analysis to see what factors could be contributing to their underperformance by analyzing performance on the last five assignments, attendance, and detention patterns.

A Dashboarding Process

The following section describes the dashboard creation process (termed "dashboarding"). The dashboarding practice outlined in Figure 6.8 was drawn primarily from Few (2006), Alexander (2008), and Barr (2011).

Figure 6.5. Strategic Dashboard Illustrating Use of High-Level Measures to Track Progress Against Goals for the Development of a Postsecondary Science Program Across Multiple Higher Education Institutions

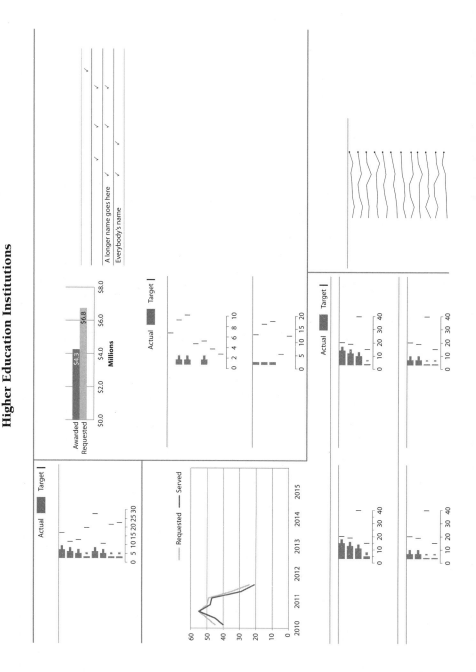

**Figure 6.6. Analytical Dashboard Design for
Marketing Analysis**

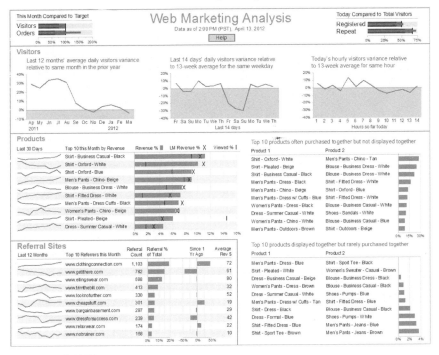

Source: Few (2013b).

Readers should also be aware that there are many other reference books for creating dashboards (e.g., Alexander & Walkenbach, 2010; Kyd, 2012; Person, 2009) and that there are even more performance measurement references that can be used to inform this process (e.g., Hatry, 2007; Hubbard, 2010; Poister, 2003).

The steps outlined in Figure 6.8 constitute a systematic process that is complementary to the evaluation process. Dashboarding begins after a need for a dashboard has been identified, stakeholder buy-in has been attained, and measures and data sources have been agreed upon and explicitly defined. Following this preparation, the evaluator will begin an iterative process as follows: 1) layout of the screen view; 2) building a dashboard using software of choice; 3) populating the dashboard with baseline data; 4) publishing the dashboard for use by stakeholders; 5) refreshing the dashboard with new data, which is followed by publishing again at an agreed-upon interval; and eventually 6) evaluating and refining the dashboard. This final step (step 6) may lead to a redesign of the dashboard if new measures are added or other measures removed. The following sections offer a more detailed description of each stage in the process.

Figure 6.7. Operational–Analytical Dashboard Design for Use by a Math Teacher to Improve Student Academic Achievement

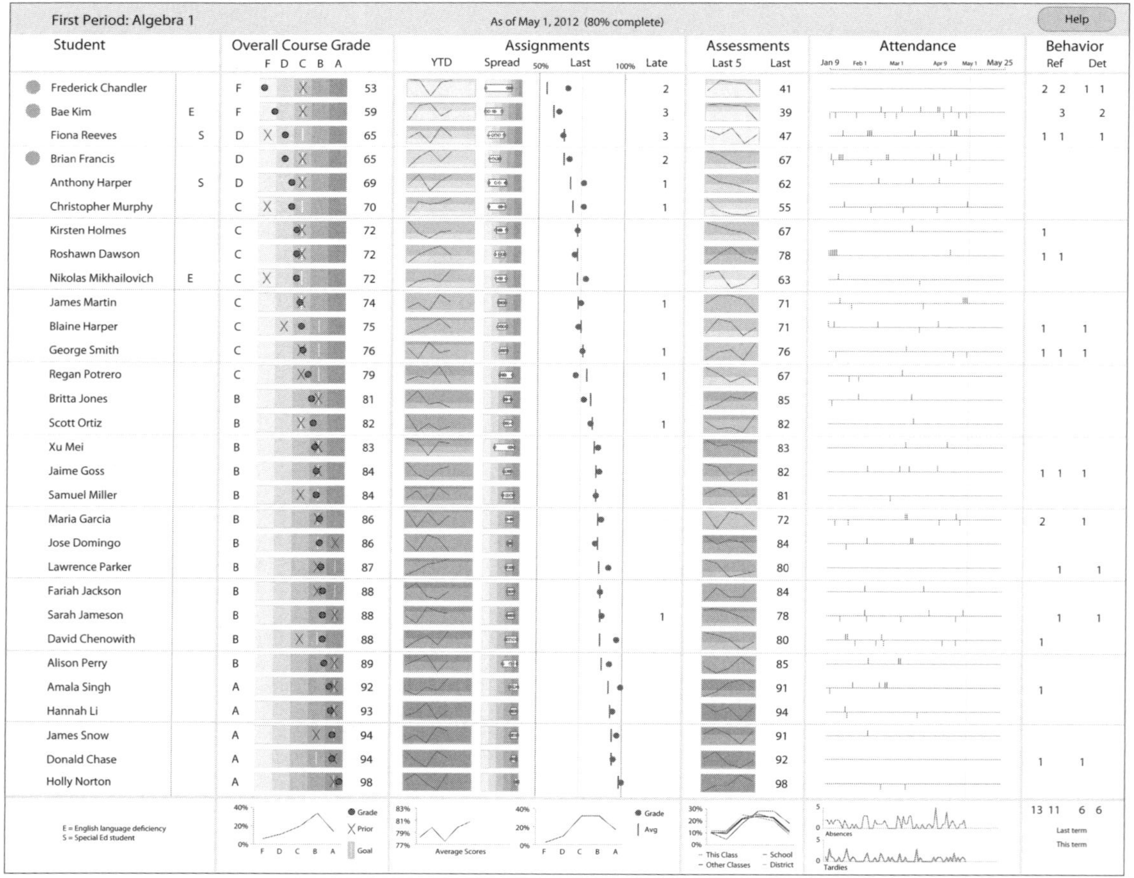

Source: Few (2013a).

Figure 6.8. Dashboarding: A Process for Creating, Using, and Maintaining Dashboards

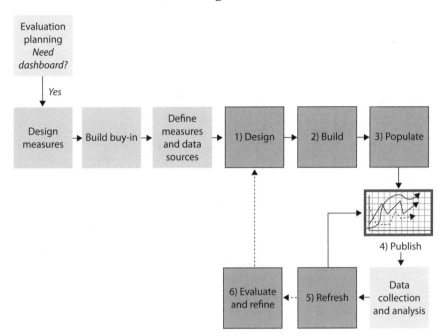

1. Design

After measures and definitions have been agreed upon and with sample data in hand, the dashboard is ready to be designed. The design constitutes the layout of the screen view (also called the presentation layer) that stakeholders will see when using the tool. The layout can be created in any number of ways, from hand sketching to detailed mockups using software packages like Adobe Illustrator or Photoshop. Microsoft Excel is commonly used for creating dashboards and is a great place to start with dashboard design.

A well-designed dashboard will add value by (Brath & Peters, 2004; Hovis, 2002):

• Transforming data repositories into consumable information
• Supporting visual identification of trends, patterns, and anomalies
• Guiding stakeholders toward effective decision making and action
• Helping people think in ways that will result in learning improvement
• Serving as a tireless, adaptable mechanism for information flow

Whether a dashboard is effective depends on its ability to deliver the necessary information to the intended audience clearly and concisely with

NEW DIRECTIONS FOR EVALUATION • DOI: 10.1002/ev

Figure 6.9. Dashboard Fragmenting Data, Which Undermines Viewers' Ability to Make Comparisons and See Relationships

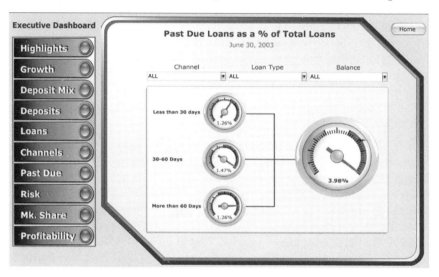

primarily visual displays. Some of the most challenging aspects of dashboard design and suggestions for overcoming those challenges are highlighted below.

A. Why a Single Screen? Although limiting the definition of a dashboard to a single screen may at first seem arbitrary, it is actually based in an understanding of human brain function and visual perception. Having everything to monitor within a single eye span enables the user to make comparisons, evaluate, and draw conclusions that are not possible when data are fragmented onto separate screens or when scrolling is required (Few, 2006). For example, as seen in Figure 6.9, the dashboard fragments data in a way that undermines bank executives' ability to see the measures together, make comparisons, and understand relationships. This design defeats one of the main aims of a dashboard, *which is to see everything you need at a glance.* Splitting the big picture into a series of small snapshots is typically a mistake in dashboard design. When viewers cannot see all the dashboard measures without scrolling, they would be better off reading a printed report across several pages, where they can be viewed all at once.

Contrast this design with Few's dashboard design in Figure 6.7 to see the power of a design that supports meaningful comparisons to inform decisions and actions that will achieve desired results.

B. Select and Design Appropriate Displays. Choosing the wrong data display is one of the most common visual design mistakes made in quantitative data presentation (Few, 2006). Misuse of pie charts is a common problem on dashboards. Pie charts are intended to display parts of a whole. However, beyond that, a pie chart does not display quantitative data effectively. Humans are not good at comparing two-dimensional areas or angles (the means that pie charts use to encode data) accurately (Few, 2006). Bar graphs more effectively communicate quantitative data. The matrix in Figure 6.10 provides a guide for selecting appropriate graphs, depending on the relationship you want to communicate.

The third row shows both lines and bars are appropriate for comparing parts to the whole. Once the appropriate graph is selected, it must be designed for the specific measure. Note that gauges are not listed on this matrix. Although gauges and meters are seemingly ubiquitous on dashboards, Few (2006, p. 125) asks the key question when considering their use: "Do they provide the clearest, most meaningful representation of the data in the least amount of space?" Radial gauges tend to waste space, because of their circular shape. This problem is magnified when multiple gauges are used. Gauges are typically used to display a single key measure and compare it to a target or within a quantitative range that illustrates the measure's state (e.g., bad, good, satisfactory). Few (2006) invented the bullet graph (Figure 6.11, top display) specifically for dashboards. The bullet graph provides the same information as the gauge in a linear format that can be oriented vertically or horizontally and can be stacked in a relatively small space. Think about how much real estate this can save on your dashboard—a key factor to consider when designing your dashboard is to get all the information needed onto one screen.

C. Usability Testing. Before beginning the build process it is important to determine if a dashboard design effectively communicates to stakeholders. Stakeholders should be asked the following evaluation questions upon viewing the initial dashboard design:

- Can you evaluate what is going on?
- Is it easy to spot the areas that need attention?
- Does the dashboard provide enough context?
- Is it easy to make sense of how the dashboard is organized?

Notice that the question, "Do you like it?" is not on this list of questions. Our intent is not to evaluate stakeholders' aesthetic preferences. Instead, we wish to evaluate the effectiveness of the dashboard to increase understanding, communicate effectively, and inform decision making. An example of how dashboard designers can go down a path of poor design because of a lack of understanding about the ideal relationship between

Figure 6.10. A Guide for Appropriate Graph Selection

Graph Selection Matrix

	Value-Encoding Objects			
Featured Relationships	Points	Lines	Bars	Boxes
Time Series Values display how something changed through time (yearly, monthly, etc.)	Yes (as a *dot plot*, when you don't have a value for every interval of time)	Yes (to feature overall trends and patterns and to support their comparisons)	Yes (vertical bars only, to feature individual values and to support their comparisons)	Yes (vertical boxes only, to display how a distribution changes through time)
Ranking Values are ordered by size (descending or ascending)	Yes (as a *dot plot*, especially when the quantitative scale does not begin at zero)	No	Yes	Yes (to display a ranked set of distributions)
Part-to-Whole Values represent parts (proportions) of a whole (for example, regional portions of total sales)	No	Yes (to display how parts of a whole have changed through time)	Yes	No
Deviation The difference between two sets of values (for example, the variance between actual and budgeted expenses)	Yes (as a *dot plot*, especially when the quantitative scale does not begin at zero)	Yes (when also featuring a time series)	Yes	No
Distribution Counts of values per interval from lowest to highest (for example, counts of people by age intervals of 10 years each)	Yes (as a *strip plot*, to feature individual values)	Yes (as a *frequency polygon*, to feature the overall shape of the distribution)	Yes	Yes (when comparing multiple distributions)
Correlation Comparison of two paired sets of values (for example, the heights and weights of several people) to determine if there is a relationship between them	Yes (as a *scatter plot*)	No	Yes (as a *table lens*, especially when your audience is not familiar with *scatter plots*)	No
Geospatial Values are displayed on a map to show their location	Yes (as bubbles of various sizes on a map)	Yes (to display routes on a map)	No	No
Nominal Comparison A simple comparison of values for a set of unordered items (for example, products, or regions)	Yes (as a *dot plot*, especially when the quantitative scale does not begin at zero)	No	Yes	No

www.PerceptualEdge.com   Derived from the book *Show Me the Numbers*   © Stephen Few 2004-2012

Source: Few (2012b).

aesthetics and use is when they hesitate to use the same type of data display (e.g., bar graph) multiple times on a single dashboard. Often I hear comments from designers like, "I think it would be good to mix it up a bit," or "I don't want users to be bored," to justify the use of a different type of graph. If a new data display is added to a dashboard just to spice things up, the dashboard design will suffer. Few (2006, p. 63) calls this "introducing

Figure 6.11. Data Displays of the Same Measures: Bullet Graphs (Top Display) Provide Clearer Data Encoding in a Small Amount of Space Compared to Gauge Graphs (Bottom Display)

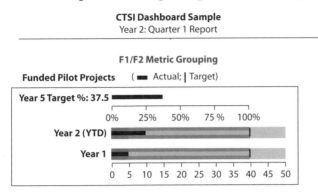

CTSI Dashboard Sample Year 2: Quarter 1 Report

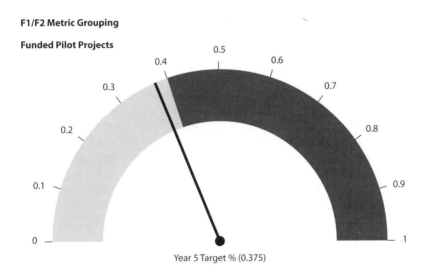

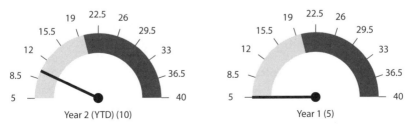

meaningless variety." Data display selection should always be based on what display is optimal for the given measure. The real design concern should be that data displays presented in an arbitrary way will frustrate viewers because they will have to work harder to get the information they need.

When testing a dashboard for usability, it is important to present stakeholders with a single prototype of the most effective design you can come up with as a starting point, as opposed to showing several options. Explain why you have selected the data displays for each of the measures and provide simple instruction for how displays (e.g., bullet graphs) that may be unfamiliar work. Provide the evaluation questions listed above and observe as the stakeholders review the dashboard and make sense of the information.

2. Build

Although dashboard design essentially amounts to a mockup of what the user will view, the build involves development of the dashboard into a working tool using software (e.g., Microsoft Excel, Tableau).The coding and organization of dashboard layers necessary to make the tool work is what I call "the build." Evaluators have many business intelligence (BI) software packages from which to choose when considering what technology to use for constructing a data dashboard, such as SAS Institute, Tableau, and Spotfire. That said, many effective and well-designed dashboards are built with the use of Microsoft Excel.

Two of Excel's greatest strengths are flexibility and ubiquity. When building a dashboard in Excel, build spreadsheets to import, aggregate, and shape data that will feed the dashboard display. Alexander (2008) calls this a data model. Building an effective model requires thinking about the dashboard from end to end. Alexander (2008) asks these questions to inform the data model: "Where will you get the data? How should the data be structured? What analysis will need to be performed? How will the data be fed to the dashboard? How will the dashboard be refreshed?" (p. 24). Although the answers to these questions will be specific to each situation, the model outlined in this section is a framework that can be used for most dashboard builds.

A typical dashboard data model (Figure 6.12) has three layers: data, analysis, and presentation. Typically there is one data layer per measure reported on the dashboard. The data layer contains the raw data that feed the dashboard. The analysis layer is where the data are analyzed and formatted. It includes formulas and pulls data from the data layer into tables. This layer is the staging area for data that are fed to the presentation layer that the viewer will see and interact with. Often the presentation layer is called the front layer, and the data and analysis layers are referred to as back layers or *backend*. Build will vary depending on the software used. For example, one can use Tableau for the presentation layer, and Excel (or Microsoft Access) for the backend. One can also build the presentation layer in Excel and link that to Access or other types of database backends.

Figure 6.12. Typical Dashboard Build Model

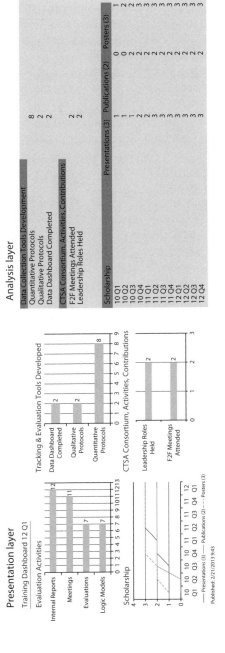

The build is the most technical part of creating a dashboard. I recommend an iterative process that includes the following steps:

(a) **Request real data.** If it does not yet exist, ask stakeholders to provide dummy data. This will improve dashboard utility and reduce the number of testing iterations needed to create a beta version of the dashboard.

(b) **Lay out the data layer in partnership with the person(s) responsible for data collection.** This is the step where data entry categories are established and data entry is specified (e.g., drop-down menu, numeric, text). Thus, engaging those who will be entering data is important.

(c) **Test data layer population with individuals who will be using the tool and encourage them to find bugs and identify issues.** Where appropriate, users should be given drop-down menus that require them to choose from predefined options. This will reduce data entry errors and will ensure consistency.

(d) **Plan for at least three iterations to finalize each data layer.** Iteration One is for reviewing the initial layout. Iteration Two involves stakeholders practicing data entry. Iteration Three typically is a population and refresh training with those who will be using, populating, and refreshing the dashboard.

3. Populate

Populating a dashboard means that the full data are entered into data layer cells for the first time. At the point of population, the dashboard will typically have been through at least two iterations of testing. Stakeholders, evaluators, and/or researchers can participate in dashboard population. A population and refresh protocol should be developed (see step five for more detail about this protocol). This protocol includes identifying who is responsible for entering data, conducting quality assurance checks, and stewarding the dashboarding process. It also outlines where and how data are to be stored and archived.

4. Publish

Publishing the dashboard is when the dashboard is shared with stakeholders electronically or in hard copy. A dashboard is typically published at a predetermined refresh interval. However, the concept of publishing does not apply to an operational dashboard that has a 1-second (or less) refresh rate. In that case, the dashboard is always live. Dissemination of dashboards can be done in a variety of ways—via the cloud, PDF, media readers (e.g., Tableau Reader), or hard copy. Operational and analytical dashboards are typically viewed via a server, allowing for dynamic access to data. Strategic dashboards are typically a snapshot in time, thus are more likely to be disseminated as a PDF or via Web or media reader with limited drill-down and hover-over functionality. The method of dissemination is an important dashboard design feature and should be determined early on in the evaluation planning stage.

5. Refresh

Refreshing a dashboard means updating the data to show the latest information available. The refresh rate indicates how frequently the dashboard is updated (e.g., every minute, day, week, month, etc.). Quarterly dashboard reporting is becoming more common with social sector organizations wanting to inform their Boards of Directors more strategically and analyze program data more frequently in order to use information formatively and summatively. Creating a refresh protocol is critical to dashboard quality. There is no faster way to blunt the use of a dashboard than to have inaccurate or outdated data.

A refresh protocol should include the following elements:

- Software and hardware requirements for viewers and those tasked with refreshing the dashboard
- Explanation of dashboard organization, including all the layers with which users will interact
- Steps for data entry, including explanation of all drop-down menu selections, and other cells that have specific data entry requirements
- Steps for the dashboard steward to follow when importing new data into the dashboard, conducting quality assurance, and publishing the dashboard
- A map of the publication and refresh process (see Figure 6.13)

6. Evaluate and Refine

In order for a dashboard to guide stakeholders toward effective decision making and action, it must be responsive to their ongoing and changing monitoring needs. It is helpful to use the analogy of application design and development (e.g., Google Maps, iTunes) when thinking about evaluating and refining dashboards over time. Assuming dashboard measures have been adequately defined and have the necessary stakeholder buy-in, a dashboard can be used for 6–12 months before its effectiveness should be evaluated and its measures reviewed. When rolling out a dashboard for the first time, I often refer to it as a "beta" version. At the 6–12-month time period, I schedule an evaluation of the dashboard with stakeholders and once again ask the questions outlined in Step 1. We also review the individual measures to assess their usefulness. At this point, design and definition of new measures may be appropriate, which would require a redesign of the dashboard

Figure 6.13. Publication and Refresh Protocol Map Example

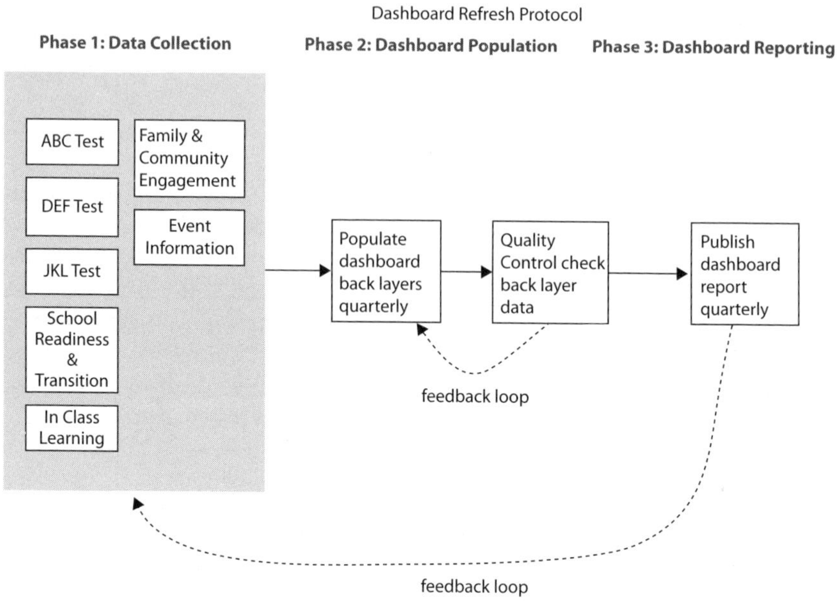

Dashboard Refresh Protocol

Phase 1: Data Collection   **Phase 2: Dashboard Population**   **Phase 3: Dashboard Reporting**

ABC Test	Family & Community Engagement
DEF Test	
	Event Information
JKL Test	
School Readiness & Transition	
In Class Learning	

Populate dashboard back layers quarterly

Quality Control check back layer data

Publish dashboard report quarterly

feedback loop

feedback loop

(and the six-step process begins again). The refined or redesigned dashboard that is the result of this step in the process would then be "Dashboard 1.0." In Figure 6.1, notice that some of the measures on the dashboard are labeled "in progress." These measures will be defined and added in future evaluation and refine phases.

Dashboard Limitations

As with any communication tool, I encourage evaluators to consider carefully whether a dashboard is the appropriate tool for the job. Dashboards should typically be avoided in the following situations.

1. Lack of Measure Design and/or Definition

Prior to creating a dashboard, the measures that are to be included on the dashboard should be designed, defined, and agreed upon by stakeholders (Steps 1–3 in Figure 6.8). In Barr's performance measurement process, called PuMP®, a performance measure is defined as "a comparison that provides objective evidence of the degree to which a performance result is occurring over time" (Barr, 2012, paragraph 3). Measure design is the part of the process that makes sure we are doing the right thinking to identify the best measures. Designing such a measure is an analytical process that begins by asking: What is one important result implied by a desired output or outcome (from the evaluation plan)? A good measure is one that is specific, can

Figure 6.14. Measure Design Template

measure design

begin with the end in mind	• [write down the result you want to measure] • [write what you want to create, not what you want to avoid]		
be sensory specific	• [what would people see, hear, feel or do if this outcome were actually happening?] • [avoid using inert language like "enhanced" or "effective" or "accountable"– use sensory-rich language as it will be easier to design measures for] • [revise your list when you are done, to remove duplicates and to keep only the sensory statements that best collectively describe your result]		
find potential measures	*potential measures*	*S*	*F*
	1. [go back to the 'be sensory specific' section and list the things you could potentially physically count as evidence of the outcome]		
	2. [for each piece of evidence you list, rate its strength relative to your outcome, and its feasibility in being brought to life, as High, Medium or Low]		
	3.		
	4.		
	5.		
	6.		
	7. [to insert more rows, click your mouse outside of the right-hand end of the row ABOVE this one, and hit your enter key]		
check the bigger picture	• [what could be the unintended consequences of achieving this outcome?] • [can you successfully prevent or manage these consequences, or do you need to revise your result/outcome?]		
name the measure(s)	• choose the measure above that rated highest for both strength and feasibility – aim for only 1, 2 or at most 3 measures • decide what to call the measure, being informative and succinct, and describe it in a sentence to make its meaning clear		

Source: Barr (2011).

be calculated, offers consistent feedback over time, and is countable. Barr (2011) has created a template (Figure 6.14) that can be used to design dashboard measures.

The measure definition (Figure 6.15) process can ensure that problems with three key assumptions are avoided: (a) how to calculate and/or analyze the measure (e.g., using the wrong data, the wrong analysis, charts that don't answer the question); (b) interpreting the measure (e.g., we don't know what signal we are looking for); and (c) using the measure (e.g., we don't know how to respond to the signal). The first critical aspect of measure definition is defining the calculation so that future analysts will know how to calculate it. Defining how to visualize the measure using line charts, bar charts, and scatter plots is another critical step. Finally, determining stakeholder response is an important and often overlooked part of measure

Figure 6.15. Measure Definition Template

name	[the name of your measure, from your measure design template]			
description	[the description of your measure, from your measure design template]			
intent	[the reason why you really need this measure, what you can't do without knowing it]			
where it fits	*level:*	[is this measure strategic, tactical or operational?]		
	result:	[which result from your impact map was this measure designed for?]		
	measure relationships:	*...is a...*	*...of measure...*	
		[cause-effect, companion, conflict]	[insert the name of the other measure this measure has strong relationships to]	
			[to insert more rows, click your mouse outside of the right-hand end of the row ABOVE this one, and hit your enter key]	
	process / department:	[which area in your organization does this measure primarily relate to?]		
calculation	*formula:*	[describe exactly how your measure's values are to be calculated, specifically identifying each data item that is required in the calculation]		
	frequency:	[how frequently should your measure's values be calculated: daily, weekly, monthly, quarterly,...?]		
	scope:	[are there any specific inclusions or exclusions from your measure?]		
	data items:	*data item name*	*description*	*source/availability*
		[to insert more rows, click your mouse outside of the right-hand end of the row ABOVE this one, and hit your enter key]		
presentation	*comparison type:*	[trend over time, point to point over time, element to element, correlation, ranking]		
	presentation method:	[choose a chart type that best displays the comparison type you need]		
	frequency:	[will your measure be presented to its audience with the same frequency as calculation, or less frequently?]		
response	[list each signal your measure could possibly give you, e.g. improvement, deterioration, no change, met target, and describe your response to each signal]			
owner(s)	*performance owner(s)*	[who is responsible for tracking this measure, interpreting its signals, and initiating action in response to those signals?]		
	data owner(s)	[who is responsible for ensuring the data is provided for this measure?]		
notes	[anything else important to document about this measure?]			

Source: Barr (2011).

definition. Stakeholders should discuss how they would interpret and use the information the measure represents (Barr, 2011).

Setting targets when defining measures assists in identifying which differences really matter. Measure definition is often the most challenging part of dashboarding because it requires developing consensus across stakeholders on exactly how the measures are to be monitored. However, without agreed-upon measure definitions, dashboard use will not facilitate productive conversations.

2. Lack of Stakeholder Buy-In for Measures and/or Dashboard

As with the practice of evaluation, leadership sponsorship and stakeholder buy-in are critical to effective dashboard use. Barr (2011) outlined a strategy called a measure gallery that has been effective at developing stakeholder support for selected measures, dashboard design, and use. Barr suggests that starting small, with performance measurement initiatives, is the key to success. Starting with one to three measures and a small group of early adopters who contribute to measure design and definition as well as dashboard design and testing can result in a dashboard that is up and running in less than 6 months. Without sufficient stakeholder buy-in, measure definition can drag on and deplete energy around the use of the dashboard. Practices that evaluators typically use for developing stakeholder buy-in can likely be adapted for dashboarding support.

3. Lack of Resources to Design and Build an Effective Dashboard

Dashboards, like any communication tool, require investment of time and money. Furthermore, dashboards are typically designed for monitoring progress against objectives over periods of time longer than a year. For these reasons, it is recommended that when designing and creating a dashboard, evaluators carefully budget for dashboarding, especially if this tool has not been used before. For example, you will need fewer resources for a dashboard with 3 measures than a dashboard with 10 or more measures. One common mistake is not allowing for enough time to design and define measures and get the sample (or dummy) data required to design the dashboard. Another mistake is not allowing enough time and money to train stakeholders in data entry, extraction, and analysis, once the tool is ready to use.

One way to reduce the time needed to create a dashboard is to simplify the major dashboard design problem: organizing multiple measures on one screen in a way that is easy to understand at a glance. Creating a dashboard report that includes only one or two measures per page simplifies this visual design problem and may be appropriate in certain situations (Figure 6.2).

4. No Want or Need to Report on the Same Measures Over Time

In these situations designing point-in-time graphs, charts, or infographics may be more appropriate than a dashboard. Recall that dashboards are about monitoring progress against goals. If there is not a monitoring need, then a dashboard is not necessary.

Conclusion

The aim of this chapter was to help evaluators and researchers optimize their use of the data dashboard as a visual communication tool. Whether designed for strategic, analytical, or operational purposes, or some combination, dashboards can improve performance measurement and monitoring for practitioners and stakeholders alike. Furthermore, the process of designing and building a dashboard is complementary to the evaluation and monitoring process. Evaluators who engage in dashboarding need facilitation skills, measurement acumen, and visual design knowledge. Evaluators can also build clients' evaluation capacity by partnering with stakeholders in the dashboarding process. Today, data dashboards and dashboard reports are becoming commonplace in evaluation and research. Evaluators and researchers are wise to determine how best to incorporate these communication tool into their practice, whether by building in-house capacity or outsourcing dashboarding expertise.

References

Alexander, M. (2008). *Excel 2007 dashboards & reports for dummies*. Hoboken, NJ: Wiley.
Alexander, M., & Walkenbach, J. (2010). *Microsoft Excel dashboards & reports*. Hoboken, NJ: Wiley.
Barr, S. (2011). *The PuMP performance measure blueprint online program*. Retrieved from http://www.performancemeasureblueprintonline.com
Barr, S. (2012). Can a milestone be a measure? Retrieved from http://www.staceybarr.com/measure-up/a-definition-of-what-a-performance-measure-really-is/
Brath, R., & Peters, M. (2004). Dashboard design: Why design is important. *Data Mining Direct*. Retrieved from http://www.information-management.com/infodirect/20041015/1011285–1.html
Butler, L. (2007). *The nonprofit dashboard: A tool for tracking progress*. Washington, DC: Boardsource.
Carman, J. G. (2007). Evaluation practice among community-based organizations research into the reality. *American Journal of Evaluation, 28*(1), 60–75.
Few, S. (2006). *Information dashboard design: The effective visual communication of data*. Sebastopol, CA: O'Reilly Media.
Few, S. (2012a). Perceptual Edge's 2012 dashboard design competition. Retrieved from http://www.perceptualedge.com/blog/?p=1308
Few, S. (2012b). *Show me the numbers: Designing tables and graphs to enlighten* (2nd ed.). Oakland, CA: Analytics Press.
Few, S. (2013a). 2012 perceptual edge dashboard design competition: A solution of my own. Retrieved from http://www.perceptualedge.com/blog/?p=1466
Few, S. (2013b). *Information dashboard design: Displaying data for at-a-glance* (2nd ed.). Oakland, CA: Analytics Press.
Hatry, H. (2007). *Performance measurement: Getting results* (2nd ed.). Washington, DC: The Urban Institute Press.

Hovis, G. L. (2002). Stop searching for information—Monitor it with dashboard technology. Data Mining Direct. Retrieved from http://www.information-management.com/infodirect/20020208/4681–1.html

Hubbard, D.W. (2010). *How to measure anything: Finding the value of intangibles in business* (2nd ed.). Hoboken, NJ: Wiley.

Kamensky, J. M. (2011). The Obama performance approach. *Public Performance and Management Review, 35*(1), 133–148.

Kaplan, R., & Norton, D. (1996). *The balanced scorecard: Translating strategy into action.* Cambridge, MA: Harvard Business School Press.

Kopczynski, M. E., & Pritchard, K. J. (2004). The use of evaluation in nonprofit organizations. In J. S. Wholey, H. P. Hatry, & K. E. Newcomer. *Handbook of practical program evaluation* (2nd ed., pp. 649–669). San Francisco, CA: Jossey-Bass.

Kyd, C. (2012). *Do you make these four mistakes with your Excel management reports?* Retrieved from http://www.exceluser.com/catalog2/ebooks/ebook.htm

McAfee, A., & Brynjolfsson, E. (2012). Big data: The management revolution. *Harvard Business Review, 90*(10), 60–68.

Newcomer, K. E. (2004). How might we strengthen evaluation capacity to manage evaluation contracts? *American Journal of Evaluation, 25*(2), 209–218.

Person, R. (2009). *Balanced scorecards & operational dashboards with Microsoft Excel.* Hoboken, NJ: Wiley.

Poister, T. H. (2003). *Measuring performance in public and nonprofit organizations.* San Francisco, CA: Jossey-Bass.

Thierauf, R. J. (1991). *Executive information systems: A guide for senior management and MIS professionals.* Westport, CT: Quorum Books.

U.S. Office of Management and Budget. (2010). Performance and management. In *President's budget for fiscal year 2011: Analytical perspectives* (pp. 71–111). Retrieved from http://www.whitehouse.gov/omb/budget/Analytical_Perspectives

VERONICA S. SMITH is a data scientist and principal of data2insight LLC, and is an expert with over 10 years of experience working with education, arts, and social service organizations.

Dean-Coffey, J. (2013). Graphic recording. In T. Azzam & S. Evergreen (Eds.), Data visualization, part 2. *New Directions for Evaluation, 140*, 47–67.

7

Graphic Recording

Jara Dean-Coffey

Abstract

*This chapter explores graphic recording, which is a visualization process that
captures the themes and ideas emerging from group discussions. This process is
well suited for many phases of an evaluation, but is particularly useful in the
initial and final stages to help the evaluator and stakeholder group explore
context and clarify focus, discuss data collection findings, and determine their
implications. The chapter provides information on what the graphic recording
process can look like and how it can fit into evaluation practice, particularly the
role that graphic recording can play in increasing cultural responsiveness and
stakeholder understanding. The chapter concludes with common questions
and answers about the graphic recording process.* © Wiley Periodicals, Inc., and
the American Evaluation Association.

jdcPartnerships would like to thank Paula Hansen (Chart Magic, http://www.chart
-magic.com) for creating the graphic illustration for this chapter as well as supporting
our evaluation work over the years. As a graphic recorder, Paula works around the
world in a variety of sectors and disciplines. She brings unique qualifications to her
work as a graphic facilitator, including a strong "right brain–left brain" balance. She has
a BA in math and art from Hamilton College in Clinton, NY, and a Masters of Fine Arts
in painting from the Maryland Art Institute in Baltimore.

Note: The figures presented in this chapter can be viewed in color by accessing www.
NDEdataviz.com and selecting Chapter 7.

G raphic recording is a technique used to capture and represent conversations visually through words and drawings. The recorder listens closely to what is being said among a group, waits, and synthesizes the conversation down to its essence. Then the recorder uses markers and pastels to write words and draw images on large paper for the group to see. Different colors and fonts differentiate mood or tone. Larger and smaller letters indicate the relative significance of an idea to participants. Icons and small drawings illustrate key ideas, and sometimes the underlying metaphor or mental model of the group is discernible as the frame for a whole mural. For example, a group that is always speaking of its trajectories, targets, and energy may be rendered with rocket ship imagery. Another group that uses the language of harvesting, growth, and sustainability may be given a farm theme. In all cases, graphic recording requires someone who can hold two ideas (or more) at one time. This skill is strengthened through training and practice. Graphic recorders are able to render through writing and drawing what was just spoken while continuing to listen ahead. The end result is a visual representation of narrative and images that captures the content of a discussion, with mental models and moods woven throughout. Because discussions often take many directions, graphic recorders must possess exceptional skills to incorporate and present spoken divergences in the context of the whole. The graphic recorder dances among spaces, words, and drawings with the movement itself reflecting the rhythm and tone of the discussion.

Generally, graphic recorders chart live and they can use either a room's smooth wall or easel(s) with white 20 lb. bond paper, usually 3 or 4 feet wide and 5 to 8 feet long or more. Graphic recorders typically engage with evaluators/consultants in two ways:

1. Graphic recorder in the room—referred to as live graphic charting (Figure 7.1). The graphic recorder and evaluator are in the room as conversations are unfolding. At the meeting's outset, the graphic recorder starts to create a mural, live and in real time, usually filling a sheet in 45–75 minutes.

2. Graphic recorder not in the room—often referred to as studio work (Figure 7.2). The graphic recorder may work with the evaluator to create frames and templates that support the evaluation process but not be in the room as a conversation unfolds. In this instance, a member of the evaluation team or even the participants might write or draw on the graphic chart.

jdcPartnerships has used both methods with equal success. The advantage of having graphic recorders in the room is their ability to support and respond to emerging conversations and themes and reflect them back to the group via words, images, conceptual frames, and metaphors. However, there are financial implications to having a graphic recorder in the room,

Figure 7.1. Live Graphic Charting

Figure 7.2. Graphic Chart (Studio Work)

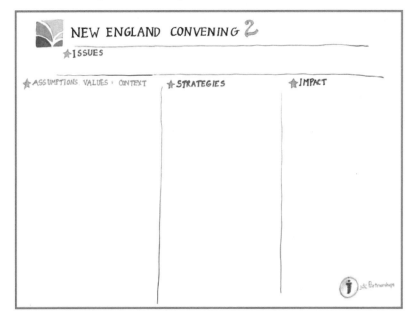

Figure 7.3. History of Graphic Recording

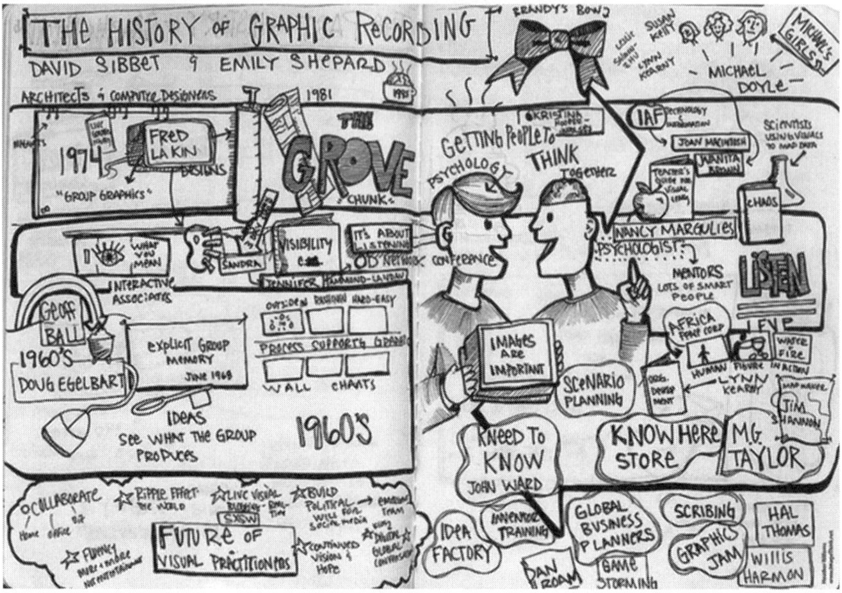

Source: Retrieved from http://ifvpcommunity.ning.com/page/who-are-we. Sketch notes by Heather Willems.

which the budget may not support. Studio work is one means to manage costs while still being able to take advantage of the skills a graphic recorder can bring to an evaluation. However, by not having them in the room and relying on premade templates, emerging frames and metaphors will be limited to the evaluation team's skills.

Graphic recording is a field that has emerged from practice (Figure 7.3), not from academia. There is little theory or written guidance for practitioners. Instead, the practice is more like a guild, usually learned by apprenticeship and advanced by mentoring. Most graphic recorders belong to an association called the International Forum of Visual Practitioners (IFVP). Training is provided during their annual meetings with presentations and papers helping fledgling graphic recorders learn the trade. The IFVP website (http://ifvpcommunity.ning.com) serves as an information and resource clearinghouse for the group and lists members by geography.

This work goes by a variety of names: graphic facilitation, visual recording, doodling, sketch noting, even viz thinking. It is not related to mind mapping or storyboarding, although those are tools that some evaluators might find useful. Mind mapping (Figure 7.4) is a way of rendering ideas in an outline form that uses trees and branches to show how ideas relate to one another (Buzan, 1974). Storyboarding originated in the film

Figure 7.4. Mind Map

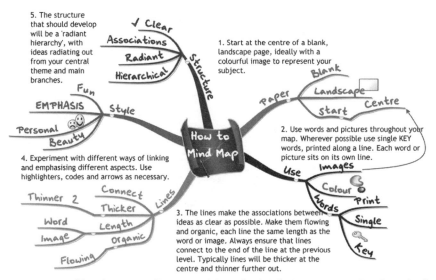

Source: Retrieved from http://www.illumine.co.uk/assimilate/mind-mapping-mastery/mind-map.html

industry and is a process for preparing a manuscript or other end product by breaking it down into "scenes" and using each cell as a container to flesh out an idea (Figure 7.5). Graphic recording differs from both of these tools in that it is nonlinear, created in the moment, and designed to support collective thinking and action while still recognizing the differing voices and perspectives of participants.

When and Why Would an Evaluator Use Graphic Recording?

Graphic recording can be used at any stage of an evaluation process, whenever people are brought together for a common purpose. As a process and a tool, its relevance and usefulness to an evaluator's work is as much a matter of personal choice and values as the determination of what types of data collection and analysis methods, presentation styles, and evaluation approaches an evaluator may include as part of his or her repertoire. That being said, it can contribute to particular evaluation approaches in unique ways, for instance, empowerment (Fetterman, Wandersman, & Millett, 2004), culturally responsive (Frierson, Hood, & Hughes, 2002), and indigenous (LaFrance, Nichols, & Kirkhart, 2012) evaluations. Additionally, the recently adopted Statement of Cultural Competence by the American Evaluation Association (AEA, 2011) provides yet another reason for evaluators to consider adding graphic recording to their toolbox.

Figure 7.5. Storyboard

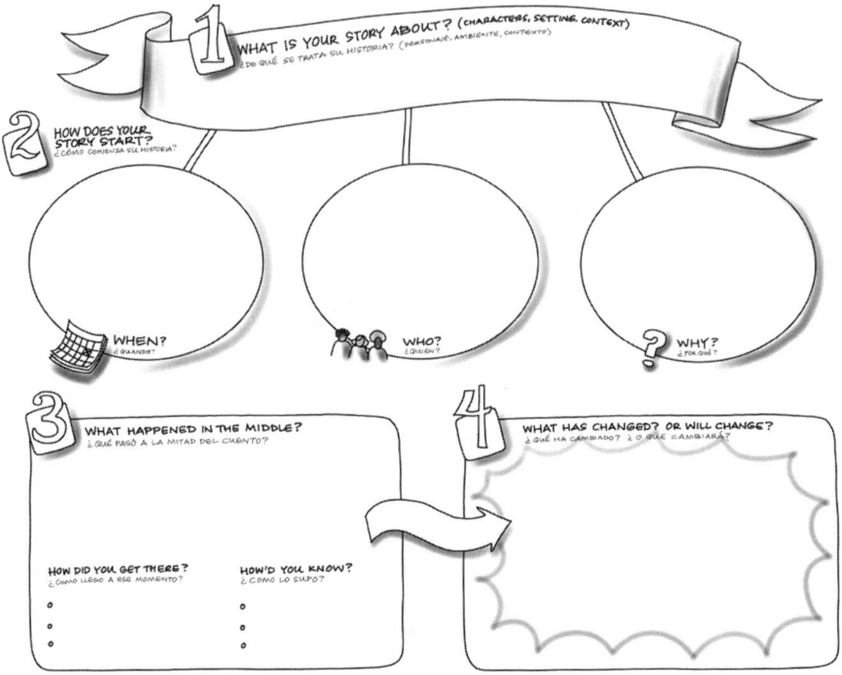

Source: Created by jdcPartnerships and RDP Consulting.

To illustrate how graphic recording can and might be adopted throughout an evaluation, the Evaluative Inquiry Cycle (Dean-Coffey, 2006) will be used as an organizing framework (Figure 7.6). Additionally, experiences with and opportunities for using graphic recording to promote particular evaluation practices will be shared. Because graphic recording is an emerging tool for evaluators, not all illustrations will be evaluation specific, but the potential application is clear.

Phase 1. Framing the Inquiry

At the onset of an evaluation, one might choose to engage the client (and whomever else) in the development of a theory of change. This is a process framed by structured questions designed to surface themes regarding core issues, values, intended changes, assumptions, context, and strategies. During this process, the graphic recorder captures the discussion and in doing so creates a visual that reflects responses, highlights themes, and reveals an emerging theory of change. This visual serves as "data" for the development of the final theory of change and provides a reference point, for those who were in the room and those who were not, about what was discussed (and what was not), so that there is a shared understanding of the ideas and exchanges that led to the theory of change.

NEW DIRECTIONS FOR EVALUATION • DOI: 10.1002/ev

Figure 7.6. Evaluative Inquiry Cycle

- **Framing the Inquiry.** Clarify the context, environment, and impetus for the work: What are the parameters for this work? What do we need to consider?

- **Focusing the Inquiry.** Identify the questions to ask and the information needed to answer them: What do we need to know and why? Who will be using the information?

- **Conducting the Inquiry.** Decide how and where the information will be obtained: How will we collect the information, now and in an ongoing manner? Where will we find it?

- **Applying the Learning.** Answer the questions: What does this mean? What should we do?

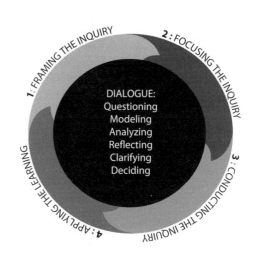

Source: Created by jdcPartnerships.

I use graphic recording most often at the onset of an evaluation engagement when we are framing the work, making assumptions explicit, creating a shared context, and focusing the evaluation effort, usually at an organizational or initiative level. For example, to set the stage for the development of an organization-wide evaluation framework, a graphic recorder worked in partnership with our team to support the development of a draft theory of change over a 2-day retreat with approximately 30 people in the room. During that period, the graphic recorder captured the discrete, structured conversations that were part of creating the draft language of the theory of change. Figure 7.7 is an example of one such conversation and the themes that emerged.

As the conversations concluded and preliminary decisions were made about various components of the theory of change, the graphic recorder created a template to help guide the discussion and development of these components (Figure 7.8).

In another half-day session, the working theory of change was shared with the Board of Directors, who were able to see and engage with it fullscale. Photographs of the original charts were shared with the Board of Directors to provide context and a visual reference for their own deliberation. Through the course of the Board of Directors' retreat, the evaluator made additions to the theory of change on the graphic record. The final paper graphic record was used as reference for creating an electronic version (Figure 7.9) that continues to serve as the foundation for the evaluation framework in the organization.

Figure 7.7. Theory of Change Values Conversation

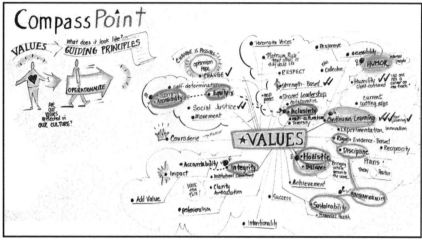

Source: Created by Paula Hansen.

Figure 7.8. Theory of Change Template

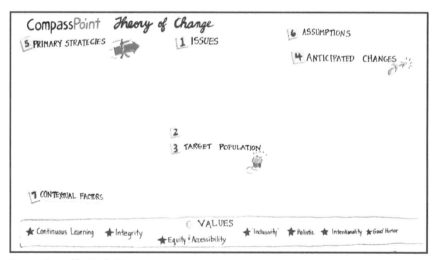

Source: Created by Paula Hansen.

In a similar engagement with a different organization, director-level staff, members of the Board of Directors, and key stakeholders (i.e., partners, funders, etc.) were in the same room for two 4-hour sessions over the course of 3 weeks. This group was charged with drafting an initial theory of change that the full Board of Directors and staff would review and revise. A graphic recorder supported both sessions by charting live as the conversations

Figure 7.9. Draft Theory of Change

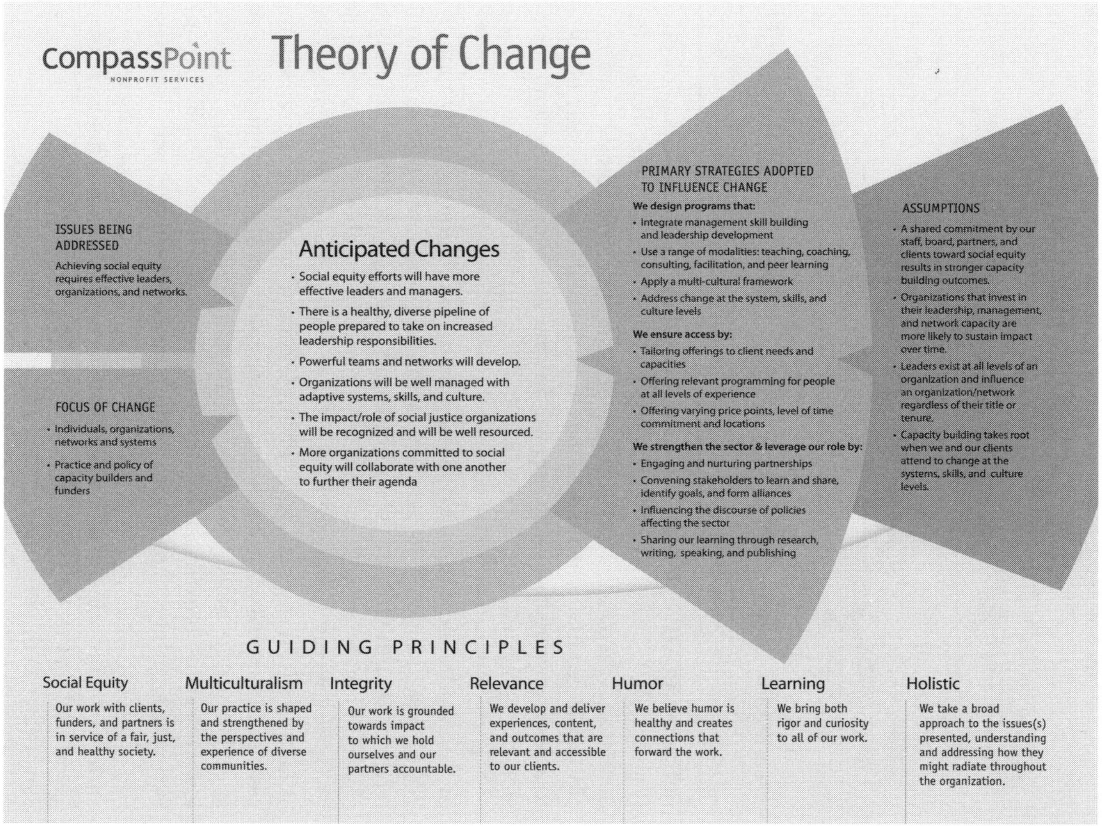

CompassPoint
NONPROFIT SERVICES

Theory of Change

ISSUES BEING ADDRESSED

Achieving social equity requires effective leaders, organizations, and networks.

FOCUS OF CHANGE

- Individuals, organizations, networks and systems
- Practice and policy of capacity builders and funders

Anticipated Changes

- Social equity efforts will have more effective leaders and managers.
- There is a healthy, diverse pipeline of people prepared to take on increased leadership responsibilities.
- Powerful teams and networks will develop.
- Organizations will be well managed with adaptive systems, skills, and culture.
- The impact/role of social justice organizations will be recognized and will be well resourced.
- More organizations committed to social equity will collaborate with one another to further their agenda

PRIMARY STRATEGIES ADOPTED TO INFLUENCE CHANGE

We design programs that:

- Integrate management skill building and leadership development
- Use a range of modalities: teaching, coaching, consulting, facilitation, and peer learning
- Apply a multi-cultural framework
- Address change at the system, skills, and culture levels

We ensure access by:

- Tailoring offerings to client needs and capacities
- Offering relevant programming for people at all levels of experience
- Offering varying price points, level of time commitment and locations

We strengthen the sector & leverage our role by:

- Engaging and nurturing partnerships
- Convening stakeholders to learn and share, identify goals, and form alliances
- Influencing the discourse of policies affecting the sector
- Sharing our learning through research, writing, speaking, and publishing

ASSUMPTIONS

- A shared commitment by our staff, board, partners, and clients toward social equity results in stronger capacity building outcomes.
- Organizations that invest in their leadership, management, and network capacity are more likely to sustain impact over time.
- Leaders exist at all levels of an organization and influence an organization/network regardless of their title or tenure.
- Capacity building takes root when we and our clients attend to change at the systems, skills, and culture levels.

GUIDING PRINCIPLES

Social Equity	Multiculturalism	Integrity	Relevance	Humor	Learning	Holistic
Our work with clients, funders, and partners is in service of a fair, just, and healthy society.	Our practice is shaped and strengthened by the perspectives and experience of diverse communities.	Our work is grounded towards impact to which we hold ourselves and our partners accountable.	We develop and deliver experiences, content, and outcomes that are relevant and accessible to our clients.	We believe humor is healthy and creates connections that are forward the work.	We bring both rigor and curiosity to all of our work.	We take a broad approach to the issues(s) presented, understanding and addressing how they might radiate throughout the organization.

Figure 7.10. Emerging Theory of Change

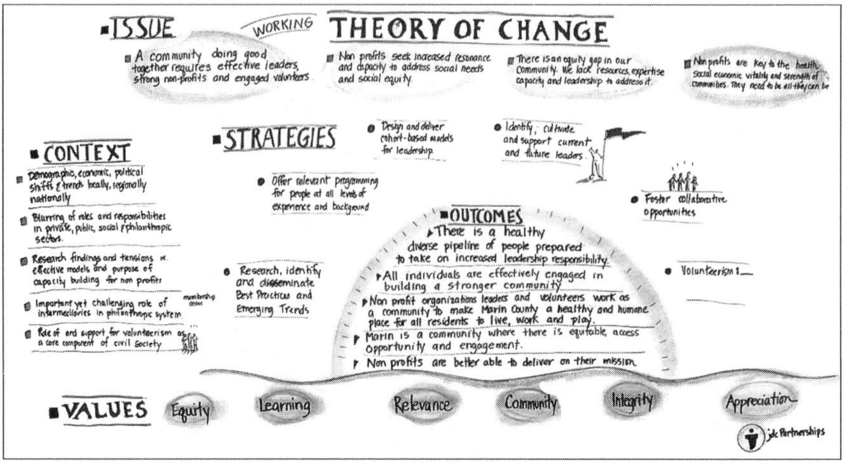

unfolded and transferred language into the emerging theory of change (Figure 7.10). The draft was reviewed by Board and staff members independently and then collectively. It has been refined and transitioned into an electronic version, which continues to be revised. It is currently being used to assess program alignment and will inform subsequent programming decisions and an evaluation framework.

Both of these examples support 2 of the 10 principles of empowerment evaluation: community knowledge[1] and inclusion[2] (Fetterman et al., 2004). The design of the sessions with the graphic recorder supported an environment in which new and different ways of describing, defining, and sharing knowledge were co-created as part of a collaborative process among those in a room. Co-created knowledge has particular resonance in non-Western cultures, where ways of knowing and being are ingrained, intuitive, and often based on holistic and natural frames of reference that can be at odds with the ways in which evaluation traditionally defines and accepts knowing. With regard to inclusion, one of the benefits of graphic recording is that it has the potential (depending on how well the evaluator designs the group process) to create a shared experience and expression with a variety of stakeholders. By its very nature, it is a platform that increases the likelihood that all voices in the room are heard (and seen) and, in doing so, can surface commonalities as well as differences.

Additionally, in the second example, by including Board, staff, and funder in the process, live graphic recording helped "recognize the dynamics of power," an element of the AEA Cultural Competence Statement (2011, p. 2). Words often serve as markers of position and power. Images and metaphors can provide a visual depiction of terms, ideas, and concepts in a landscape void of internalized or externalized expressions of power and role. Although this can be part and parcel of any program design and its subsequent evaluation, for the purposes of this discussion it speaks to the relationship between evaluator, client, and others engaged in the evaluation process. Forethought and planning are needed to incorporate graphic recording meaningfully into an evaluation process. Evaluators who understand, practice, and value group process can also be skilled facilitators who create environments that seek to treat all voices equally.

Using graphic recording during this initial stage of evaluation can act as a leveler because it is not something with which most people are familiar. Because it is not widely used, it is seen as something new and interesting that can change the energy when participants are talking about evaluation-related issues that those in the room may not be keen to discuss.

Phase 2. Focusing the Inquiry

As part of the process to determine areas of interest for the evaluation, graphic recording can help organize a brainstorm in a way that surfaces priority inquiry areas by grouping similar questions into "families." This can support further discussion of sources and methods, as well as potential challenges and opportunities, to move the inquiry forward.

jdcPartnerships was able to use live graphic recording in our work with an organization exploring not only its own effectiveness but also ways in which it might reconfigure in the future in order to better leverage strengths and increase adaptability. To facilitate the discussion, participants were asked to respond to four questions that provided the frame for the graphic recording:

1. What characteristics have supported progress to date?
2. In what areas do we have a unique competency (i.e., content areas and strategies)?
3. What gaps in the current system can we address?
4. Who do we see as our critical partners?

The ensuing dialogue captured by the graphic recorder (Figure 7.11) led to a discussion about potential roles (Figure 7.12) that served as the inquiry frame for the research that jdcPartnerships conducted, and resulted in an article identifying potential models and considerations for the organization to explore.

Phase 3. Conducting the Inquiry

Among the data collection tools most often used in evaluation are interviews or focus groups. These may not always be the most appropriate data collection methods given culture and context. Instead, graphic recording can be used to support a facilitated dialogue, led by an evaluator, among a group of people (e.g., study participants, stakeholders) on a single or variety of topics. In doing so, themes can emerge by the way in which they are

Figure 7.11. Determining Research Agenda: Potential Roles

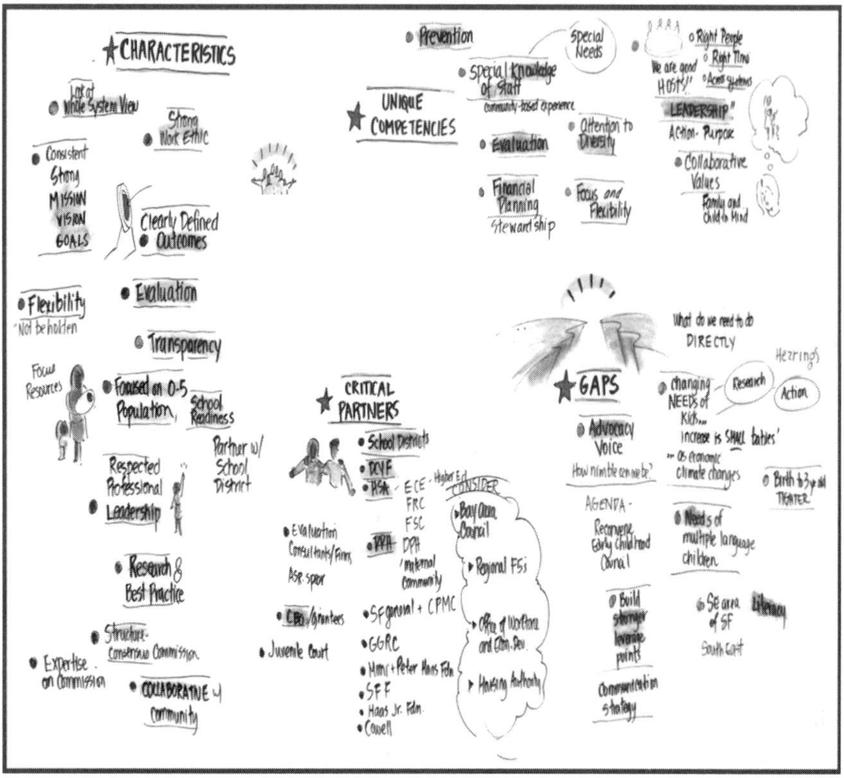

Source: Created by Paula Hansen.

reflected on a mural chart. This can advance the inquiry for an evaluator by identifying areas for additional probing and exploration both in the moment and afterward.

Phase 4. Applying the Learning

Preliminary findings can be shared with stakeholders in a process designed to use graphic recording to engage a group in "sense-making." The larger group can divide into small groups to explore findings, identify implications, suggest next steps, and then share with the full group (Figure 7.13).

The graphic recorder would capture the organizing patterns and reveal areas of agreement, variance, and dissonance. The visual representation of data and discussion can diffuse tension (due to differing perspectives or experiences) because people are not facing each other across a table but are facing a visual record that they are helping to create together. This helps take the pressure off individuals and promotes group ownership and decision making.

Figure 7.12. Context and Organizational Strengths Discussion

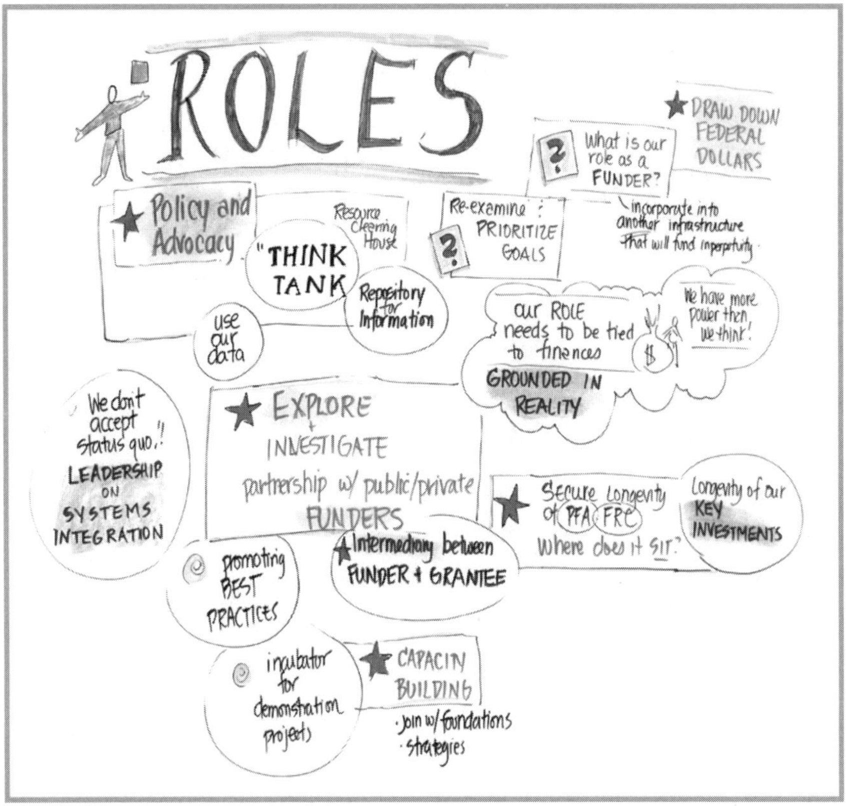

Source: Created by Paula Hansen.

The graphic record itself can then serve as a summary of dialogue, decisions, and other information, which synthesizes findings and themes in an accessible and often more concise manner for diverse individuals to use beyond the evaluation space.

How Is Graphic Recording Being Used in the Field?

There have been other published examples of the use of graphic recording to support evaluation practice. One the most recent implementations of this method is Pipi's (2010) evaluation of the Planning Alternatives to Tomorrow's Health (PATH) program and the work conducted in Maori settings. PATH is based on person-centered planning, developed in the late 1980s. Grounded in the principles of capacity building, it was designed to assist individuals with disabilities to achieve their dreams and aspirations. Underlying principles are diversity and inclusion as well as an acknowledgment of the

NEW DIRECTIONS FOR EVALUATION • DOI: 10.1002/ev

Figure 7.13. Sense Making

Source: Created by Paula Hansen.

unique context and circumstance of their lives and/or culture. Pipi (2010), who frequently works with indigenous and tribal communities in Canada and New Zealand, speaks to how these principles resonate strongly with Kaupapa Maori principles and practice. PATH (through graphic recording) supports a core principle of inclusion and Pipi (2010) argues that:

> whanau the principle of inclusion promotes that all whanau members who will be affected by the PATH be included and that the collective ideas and views of all are welcomed and embraced. It means that all ages, all whanau members, all levels of expertise and experience are valuable in planning. (p. 3)

PATH uses visual images complemented by facilitation that "promotes storytelling and critical analysis as well as active engagement from stakeholders" (Pipi, 2010, p. 1). Through PATH, participants are engaged in a facilitated process that uses graphic recording to capture all the core elements of evaluation and places them visually on a pathway that reflects the cultural metaphors and images that best represent the community (Figure 7.14) (Pipi, 2010).

In this instance, graphic recording as part of the PATH model (Table 7.1) reflects elements of an indigenous evaluation framework (IEF) as well as culturally responsive evaluation (CRE) described by LaFrance et al. (2012)

Figure 7.14. PATH: Hapū and Iwi Focused

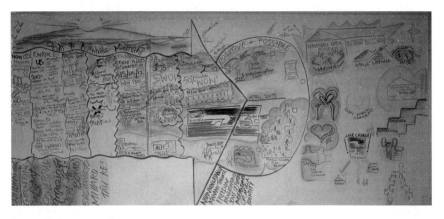

Source: Pipi (2010, p. 5).

Table 7.1. PATH/Evaluation Term Crosswalk

PATH Components	Evaluation Terms
Dreams and aspirations	Outcome
The setting of goals	Establishing outputs
Where we are now in relationship to those goals	Baseline data
Who needs to be enrolled to provide support and areas that need to be strengthened	Capability and capacity
Action planning	Measurable indicators

and Frierson et al. (2002), respectively. IEF places context at the core of an evaluation and in doing so forces the reconceptualization of methods and epistemology that for the most part have been sacred in evaluation. It emphasizes metaphor and story as essential components of the design and implementation of evaluation—something that graphic recording can help to express and represent. IEF also recognizes knowledge as living, continuing to evolve. The ability to return to a graphic chart and modify it based on new learning and contextual shifts provides a visual record of the evolution of knowledge. Graphic charts are also photographed as a matter of practice (for ease of use and reference), so before and after shots can provide historical context and grounding and show the evolution of thoughts and perspectives. This is different from updating a written report with new information in that although one might be able to use "track changes" to see the evolution of a report or add headings to organize additional narrative, the end product and the way in which a reader interacts with and experiences the document is quite different.

CRE increases the importance of culture and supports its use as a critical lens for not just understanding an evaluation but also for an evaluator's ability to work in partnership, respectfully and effectively, with a client. CRE particularly espouses the belief that an evaluator or an evaluation team must have the "shared lived" experience to hear truly what is being said. At the very least, the evaluator or evaluation team should be fully aware of and responsive to the participants' and stakeholders' culture, particularly as it relates to and influences the program (Frierson, Hood, & Hughes, 2002, p. 65).

From this perspective, cultural nuances are not explained away but are used as an explicit lens through which the data and findings are viewed. Graphic recording can be helpful in elucidating cultural norms, assumptions, and practices from stakeholder groups that may not share an evaluator's cultural background, experience, or language. Additionally, hearing only voices reduces the biasing effects of physical appearances on the judgment of a graphic recorder as words are spoken. If an idea sounds important and the graphic recorder feels the group is becoming excited about it, the idea will be given space on the mural with large letters—even if it was from a person in the room who may not traditionally be seen as having power, knowledge, and insight (groups typically marginalized in evaluation endeavors). Conversely, someone with positional authority might ramble, but if nothing new is being contributed and the graphic recorder isn't picking up any energy, he or she will wait for the next major point to be made by someone else. The impartiality of a graphic recorder permits a range of voices to be heard and considered regardless of position or leadership role (Figure 7.15).

This approach reflects the evolution of evaluation to a field that is beginning to recognize the value and importance of expertise and experience beyond that of an evaluator and the notions of empirical and objective data. It intentionally includes and honors the perspectives and knowledge of the community impacted by the program or effort in question and/or the program designers.

In the examples and scenarios presented, when intentionally integrated into the evaluative inquiry cycle, graphic recording can also assure that an evaluation process reflects three additional elements of the AEA Cultural Competence Statement (2011): culturally appropriate methods, the complexity of cultural identity, and the bias in language.

Employ Culturally Appropriate Methods

Different cultures (in the broadest sense of the word) use different means of communication. Graphic recording, with its ability to integrate both words and images to capture voice and convey meaning, can bridge the gap between ethnic communities, fields of discipline, and regional and class differences. This is particularly relevant to non-Western and indigenous/

Figure 7.15 Being Heard and Seeing Connections

Source: Created by Paula Hansen.

tribal communities, although there is cause to suspect that, for the younger Western generation that has grown up in a much more visual and interactive world, graphic recording and other visual displays may resonate more than with previous generations.

Acknowledge the Complexity of Cultural Identity

Culture is not limited to ethnicity or language. It encompasses all that makes us individuals and when we gather, the complexity of culture increases. In evaluation, there are differing opinions as to whether culture is part of context or if it is in and of itself a frame by which one experiences and describes context. The use of graphic imagery can often better capture the nuances in the expression of cultures, particularly non-Western cultures, through the use of metaphors and images that reflect historical, metaphysical, spiritual, and natural expressions of meaning. Additionally, graphic recording by its very nature can make more transparent the meaningful differences and commonalities that can be important in designing an evaluation, making sense of the analytical findings, and determining implications for action and decision.

Recognize and Eliminate the Bias in Language

The use of visual and conceptual images can help a group move past and through the terms and words that often prevent understanding each other and working towards shared ends. This can be particularly true in evaluation where the jargon of the field can be a barrier to those engaged in evaluative efforts. The use of graphic recording in evaluation creates an environment where words take second stage to concepts, themes, and ideas that can create a more level playing ground for the exchange of information

and the types of dialogue that occur between and among various participants. A resulting mural created by a graphic recorder represents an integrated and collective documentation of a group discussion rather than
separate and individual musings. A graphic recorder captures the tone and
nature of the dialogue and depicts this by the way words are positioned
and drawn on a graphic chart.

And as the notions of utilization-focused evaluation (Patton, 2008) are
more broadly accepted, graphic recording as part of the evaluation toolkit
can promote more ready access to, and thus use of, evaluation findings.
This can be attributed to the fact that the graphic record is immediate.

People may be accustomed to the recording and transcribing of minutes that are returned a week or so after a meeting. This is an important
shift in power because everyone can see what is being recorded and there is
a much greater feeling of shared ownership of the findings, implications,
and next steps. Everyone has a chance to comment on, amend, or add to
what is being recorded, so that the record is accurate and really belongs
to everyone. Additionally, graphic recording boosts learning for visual and
kinesthetic learners. This is important because more and different types of
people are involved in evaluative activities with differing learning styles
and preferences.

Common Questions About Graphic Recording

What Are Some Ways the Graphic Recorder/Graphic Chart Can Be Integrated Into the Evaluation Process?

Pictures of the charts can be used as a summary of the sessions along with
a memo highlighting the process and suggesting ways to use the charts.
These pictures can also be used as reference points for discussions and decisions throughout the process. They can also be integrated into a written
report and presentation and used to communicate to different audiences.

The interpretation of these charts is also an important consideration
when using the photos. Many times the graphic recording metaphors are
fairly easy to read and understand, but it might be wise to provide the audience with additional guidance to help them see the process and the results
of the group's work. It is also worthwhile to ask graphic recorders questions
about the choice of metaphors, words, mental models, colors, font in the
actual graphic record, and if there was anything else they noticed as they
listened. The ability to understand and interpret the chart also has implications for the chart's role as a data source. Graphic recorders process in the
moment, holding past and present simultaneously, which is reflected in
the graphic chart produced live. The themes that emerge and the metaphors used are those that surface in the group process and are informed, as
all things are, by experience and values (albeit their training reinforces their

role as filter or mirror as opposed to translator). That being said, depending on their role in the evaluation process, they could be considered a data source.

What Are Some of the Limitations or Cautions of Graphic Recording as an Evaluation Tool?

Our experience with graphic recording as part of our toolkit has been positive and we continue to explore ways to incorporate it throughout the evaluative inquiry cycle. We have developed relationships with two graphic recorders over the past 7 years who have been helpful to us as we think about meaningful ways to use it that benefit the client and the process. However, several challenges surface in its use. Another person equals additional monies associated with personnel on the evaluation budget. Given that evaluation budgets overall tend to be less than the work warrants, it may not be possible to add another person to the team. Also, sometimes the client has had negative experiences with graphic recording. On more than one occasion, we have had a client say to us when we propose graphic recording, "I don't get it" or "I have seen it and it just looks like glorified note taking." But that is more the issue of the facilitator than the graphic recorder. In these instances, we often negotiate an approach where if the client does not find value in the initial session, we have a Plan B that does not include the graphic recorder.

How Would an Evaluator Engage a Graphic Recorder?

Graphic recorders who are members of IFVP.org have webpages on that site, which may be searched by geography. Depending on where an evaluator is geographically located, there may or may not be a graphic recording community. If there is not, there will be cost implications to use graphic recording in the group process. But most graphic recorders travel, so budget notwithstanding, a graphic recorder is available to accompany an evaluator anywhere. As for whether or not a graphic recorder will fit with a team, the clearer an evaluator can be about graphic recording's support to the evaluation process and the more flexible about the experiences and ideas of an individual graphic recorder, the higher the probability of a successful partnership.

What Can an Evaluator Expect?

An evaluator will likely contact a graphic recorder to describe an upcoming meeting and its purpose and desired outcomes. It's helpful to share the agenda with some initial thoughts as to where graphic recording might be useful. The graphic recorder will develop a scope of work or estimate and sign any provided confidentiality agreements. After an agreement is signed, the graphic recorder will research the topic and companies involved, learn jargon or technical terms, and research logos and other imagery associated with the firms or nature of the field. Sometimes, the graphic recorder will send quick sketches of what she thinks might work or examples from other engagements. A follow-up conversation should occur at least 1 or 2 weeks beforehand to review the agenda. The graphic recorder will want to know if there is sufficient wall space in the venue or if easels and a foam-core backboard will be required. Usually the graphic recorder needs at least 4' × 6' of unobstructed wall space.

At the end of the meeting, the graphic recorder usually takes photographs of the charts and leaves the actual charts with the evaluator (or the client). The graphic recorder will later send color electronic versions of the wall charts that can be formatted for print and web.

How Would Graphic Recording Change the Evaluation Practice?

Intentionally thinking about group process design in a way that creates space and place for voices, ideas, and concepts to be expressed in a manner that advances the discussion is an art and a skill.

For those less familiar or comfortable with group process, it might be a stretch. It is a move to appreciate more fully the qualitative elements of evaluation and develop capacity as a practitioner to create semistructured and visual methods to capture data that inform understanding of context, analysis, findings, and implications.

Additionally, working with a graphic recorder might be challenging if an evaluation practitioner is not used to working with others in a multidisciplinary team relationship. Being open to how a graphic recorder's experience and framing can strengthen the evaluation is important. This also means that an evaluator needs to be able to communicate clearly the intentions of the group process and the ways in which she hopes that graphic recording can support it.

The evolution of empowerment, culturally responsive, participatory, and other types of evaluation, which more explicitly note the value and importance of inclusion, diversity, and collaborative sense and decision making, are pushing the envelope of what should be core skills for an effective evaluator. Fortunately, there is a wide range of methods and tips for structuring dialogue, managing behavior, and moving groups forward that enhance the effectiveness of the group process. Building one's skill set and comfort in this area as an evaluator will assure that the graphic recording is seen and used as a meaningful core element of the evaluation process.

For evaluators who already have group process design and facilitation as a core part of their toolkit, graphic recording can be a great way to elevate the thinking and practice of doing so further, with another professional who brings a skill set for hearing, placing, and identifying core pieces of information to move evaluation work forward. It can actually free an evaluator to focus on the process of inquiry and engaging those in the room

NEW DIRECTIONS FOR EVALUATION • DOI: 10.1002/ev

more fully while also paying attention to themes and patterns in the interpersonal dynamics that have bearing on the work.

Endnotes

1. Organizational and community stakeholders, not evaluators, are considered to be in the best position to understand the community's problems and to generate solutions to those problems.
2. Inclusion involves the representation and participation of key stakeholders.

References

American Evaluation Association. (2011). *American Evaluation Association public statement on cultural competence in evaluation.* Fairhaven, MA: Author. Retrieved from http://www.eval.org/ccstatement.asp

Buzan, T. (1974). *Using both sides of the brain.* New York, NY: Dutton.

Dean-Coffey, J. (2006). *Evaluation inquiry cycle.* Retrieved from http://jdcpartnerships.com/PDFs/evaluative_inquiry.pdf

Fetterman, D., Wandersman, A., & Millett, R. A. (2004). *Empowerment principles in practice.* New York, NY: Guilford Press.

Frierson, H. T., Hood, S., & Hughes, G. B. (2002). Strategies that address culturally-responsive evaluation. In J. F. Westat, *The 2002 user friendly handbook for project evaluation* (pp. 63–73). Arlington, VA: National Science Foundation.

LaFrance, J., Nichols, R., & Kirkhart, K. E. (2012). Culture writes the script: On the centrality of context in indigenous evaluation. *New Directions for Evaluation, 135,* 59–74.

Patton, M. Q. (2008). *Utilization-focused evaluation* (4th ed.). Thousand Oaks, CA: Sage.

Pipi, K. (2010). *The PATH planning tool and its potential for whanau research.* Retrieved from http://www.review.mai.ac.nz/index.php/MR/article/viewFile/377/555

JARA DEAN-COFFEY is founder and principal of jdcPartnerships.

Azzam, T. (2013). Mapping data, geographic information systems. In T. Azzam & S. Evergreen (Eds.), *Data visualization, part 2. New Directions for Evaluation, 140,* 69–84.

8

Mapping Data, Geographic Information Systems

Tarek Azzam

Abstract

This chapter offers an introduction to geographic information systems (GIS) and provides examples of how this approach to data visualization can help evaluators better understand the context in which they are working, conduct a deeper analysis of the data, and communicate using maps to illustrate important findings and patterns. The chapter also discusses the limitations of this approach and offers suggestions for those interested in integrating GIS in their evaluation practice. © Wiley Periodicals, Inc., and the American Evaluation Association.

Geographic information systems (GIS) is a method of linking quantitative or qualitative data to geographic markers and locations (Chang, 2007; Renger, Cimetta, Pettrgrove, & Rogan, 2002). This ability allows evaluators to create maps that combine program information with geographic characteristics that surround them. So why is GIS a potentially important visualization approach? The best way to illustrate its relevance is through an example of a study that utilized GIS to map the locations of tobacco billboards in the St. Louis, MO, area. Luke, Esmundo,

---

Note: The figures presented in this chapter can be viewed in color by accessing www.NDEdataviz.com and selecting Chapter 7.

**Figure 8.1. Map Showing the Location of Tobacco Billboards
Overlaid on a Map Showing the Socioeconomic Distribution
of the Population**

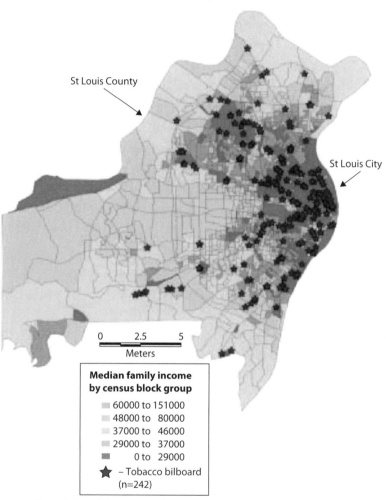

Source: Luke et al. (2000).

and Bloom (2000) collected the geographic locations of all tobacco billboards in St. Louis, and mapped those data. The locations of the tobacco
billboards were combined with other community data to create some strik-
ing and informative maps. One of these maps (Figure 8.1) overlaid the
tobacco billboard location data on top of a map showing the socioeconomic
(SES) distribution of households across St. Louis. This map illustrated a
stark pattern that suggested that tobacco billboards tended to be predomi-
nantly located in low SES communities (Figure 8.1). The authors also used
the same billboard location data and overlaid it on top of the locations of
elementary, middle, and high schools in St. Louis (Figure 8.2). This map

NEW DIRECTIONS FOR EVALUATION • DOI: 10.1002/ev

Figure 8.2. A Map Showing the Location of Public Schools (With a ½-Mile Buffer in Gray) and the Location of Tobacco Billboards

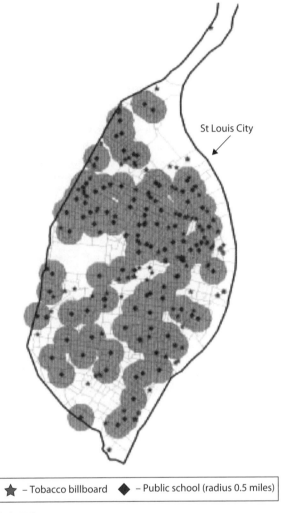

St Louis City

★ – Tobacco billboard   ◆ – Public school (radius 0.5 miles)

Source: Luke et al. (2000).

showed that 74% of all tobacco billboards were located within ½ mile of all public schools and were within easy visual range.

The causal inferences implied by these two maps will be discussed later in the chapter, but the main point is that the authors' use of these maps helped them detect patterns of interaction between the data they collected (i.e., the location of tobacco billboards) and community characteristics data (e.g., SES distribution, public school locations). These patterns may have been missed if the data were displayed in a table format or if simple charts were used instead of a GIS-generated map. This visualization

NEW DIRECTIONS FOR EVALUATION • DOI: 10.1002/ev

process can be used to conduct needs assessments, track change over time, compare multiple variables, capture and document program implementation, and understand the factors that helped or hindered the achievement of program outcomes (Azzam & Robinson, 2013). The following sections will provide more details of how GIS can be used to achieve these important evaluation tasks, along with illustrative examples.

GIS Logistics

Before delving into the role of GIS in evaluation there are a few logistical steps that will help explain how these maps were created. GIS in many of these examples utilizes a database-like system to create the maps. This means that the format of the data would look almost exactly like a database sheet in Excel or SPSS, with the only difference being the addition of some form of geographic variable such as an address, GPS coordinate, city name, street name, census block, and so on (Goodchild & Janelle, 2004). Table 8.1 contains an example of what the format might look like.

Table 8.1 contains information on the smoking habits of males and females within each country, and the country names were used as the location variable to create the maps in Figure 8.3 with the use of the website Many-Eyes.com. More advanced GIS software like ESRI's ArcGIS can easily "geocode" addresses, meaning that they can automatically transform a home address into a GPS coordinate to be mapped. This software can also be used to conduct more sophisticated geo-statistical analysis that can help evaluators make inferential claims about the relationship between environmental features and program outcomes. These types of analysis are discussed in more detail in the Azzam and Robinson (2013) article, along with a case example.

The drag-and-drop method is an easier way of creating maps and can be used with Google Maps and Bing Maps. A few of the examples provided in this chapter have utilized this method for map creation. It entails finding the location of interest (e.g., the address of program site) and selecting a marker from the Google or Bing menu and dragging that marker to the location of interest. These software applications also allow you to add unique location identifiers by changing the shape or color of the markers and additional information about each site within each of the markers (e.g., pictures, text, video, etc.).

Some states and counties also have GIS-based websites that allow users to create their own maps using publicly available data. Typically each state has a GIS office that can provide additional resources to users, although the breadth and depth of these resources vary from state to state. A few of the maps in this chapter utilized these websites to create unique maps that illustrate areas of needs and available community resources, a valuable tool for evaluators interested in using GIS in their practice.

The final logistical point is that map-scale matters a great deal when creating a GIS map. Change in map-scale often results in changes in the

Table 8.1. An Example of What a GIS Database Table Would Look Like

	Country	Population (2001)	Adult Smoking	Male Smoking	Female Smoking
1	Rwanda	7609	5.50%	7.00%	4.00%
2	Haiti	8142	9.70%	10.70%	8.60%
3	Nigeria	113862	8.60%	15.40%	1.70%
4	Oman	2538	8.50%	15.50%	1.50%
5	United Arab Emirates	2606	9.00%	18.30%	0.05%
6	Bahamas	304	11.50%	19.00%	4.00%
7	Sweden	8842	19.00%	19.00%	19.00%
8	Malawi	11308	14.50%	20.00%	9.00%
9	Australia	19138	19.50%	21.10%	18.00%
10	Saudi Arabia	20346	11.50%	22.00%	1.00%
11	Palau	19	15.10%	22.30%	7.90%
12	Bahrain	640	14.60%	23.50%	5.70%
13	Colombia	42105	22.30%	23.50%	21.00%
14	Fiji	814	20.50%	24.00%	17.00%

Source: Many-eyes.com

Figure 8.3. A GIS Map Showing the Proportion of Male and Female Smokers Across the World

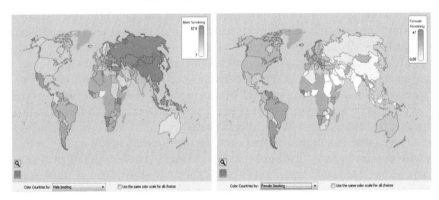

Source: Many-eyes.com

observed pattern of the results (e.g., a map created at the state level will hide details that may appear in a county- or city-level map). Scale can also affect the type of data that can be accessed and embedded within maps. Some data or variables may only be available at the state or county level, whereas others can be accessed at census tract level or even individual

NEW DIRECTIONS FOR EVALUATION • DOI: 10.1002/ev

household level. These varying scales can enable you to create maps with different levels of resolution and detail, but be aware that selecting the appropriate scale for an analysis is a critical step in this process. Scale can be determined by the program's expected impact area. For example, a program that is designed to have an impact on a neighborhood would require a map that has neighborhood-level details, whereas a program that is aimed at changing an outcome at the state level would require a state-level map. Although this may seem obvious, in practice it is sometimes difficult to find data that fit within the needed map-scale.

GIS and Program Implementation

Multisite programs can benefit from a geographic representation to help them strategically predict future areas of need and examine quality of implementation and factors affecting program fidelity. An evaluator can work with programs to create a tailored community needs assessment map that depicts areas of need and the resources available to serve those needs. Figure 8.4 shows a map created using a publicly available GIS database (obtained from http://www.healthycity.org). This map shows the distribution of adults with no high school diploma across a specific region in Southern California. The darker regions of the map represent areas with a high concentration of adults with no high school diplomas. Overlaid on top of this map are the locations of all adult schools (represented by circles) that serve the needs of individuals with no high school diploma. An examination of Figure 8.4 reveals service gaps where there are dark areas of land and few circles, notably concentrated at the bottom right corner. This needs assessment map can help adult school programs identify future service locations and show how existing resources are being optimally distributed across a specific geographic region.

A simpler GIS map can also be created to track each program site's unique characteristics and information (Figure 8.5). This provides the program and the evaluator with an overview of each site and can be used to embed information about the site, the population it serves, its upcoming events, and the capacity remaining at each location. The evaluator and client can easily update this information through Google Maps and use it as a communication tool for interested stakeholders. These types of maps can also be used to track program implementation by embedding information on various program activities and examining whether there are discrepancies by location or time across the different sites.

These maps can also be created for more complex initiatives that have different multisite programs and can be used to show the connections and networks that are formed across these differing programs. For example, I conducted an evaluation of a college recruitment initiative that contained many subprograms operating in the same general geographic area. One of the difficulties with evaluating this program was understanding how the

Figure 8.4. A Map Showing the Distribution of Adults With no High School Diplomas and the Location of Adult Education Schools

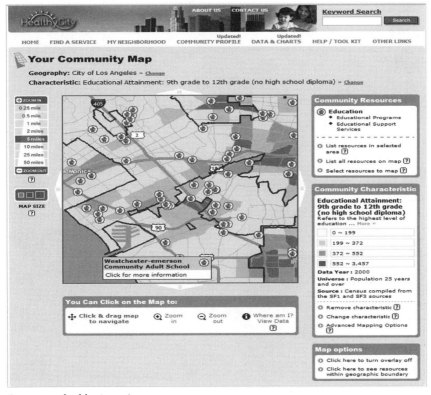

Source: www.healthycity.org/

Figure 8.5. An Example of a Map Containing Program Location and Descriptions

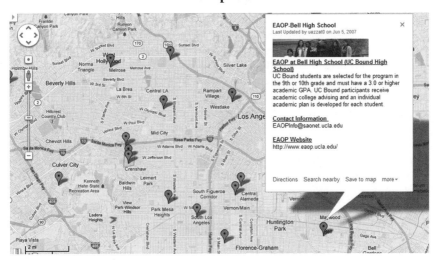

Source: www.maps.google.com

Figure 8.6. An Example of a Map Showing Connections Between Program Sites

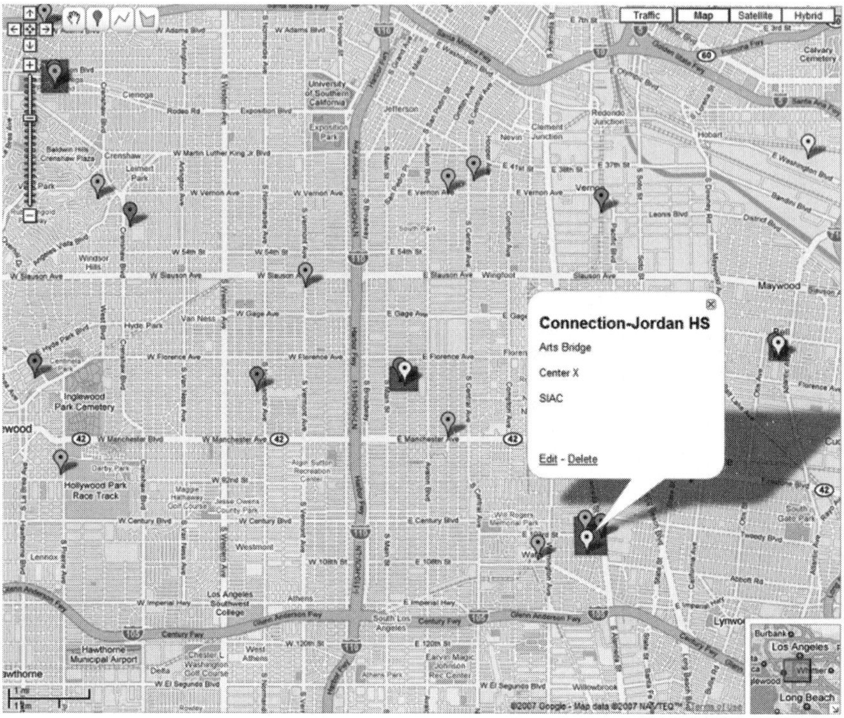

Source: www.maps.google.com

initiatives and the programs worked together toward the common objective of getting more high school students into college. I contacted each program and asked them to report the names of the schools in which they were working. I used that information to create a map (Figure 8.6) showing the location of each of the different subprograms (each program had a different colored marker), and we discovered that a few of the subprograms were actually operating within the same schools without being aware of each other. This map helped the initiative directors view the spread of the various subprograms and identify the connection between them. This effort led to more collaboration among subprograms and a reduction in replication of services.

More complex GIS maps can be used to track barriers or supporting factors to program implementation by representing environmental conditions affecting program fidelity. For example, an evaluator could create a map representing program enrollment or attendance at each site. This data could be overlaid with the location of transit lines, crime statistics, parking availability, or a host of other community characteristics. Such a map was

NEW DIRECTIONS FOR EVALUATION • DOI: 10.1002/ev

Figure 8.7. An Example of a Map Showing the Location of Students, Schools, and Transportation Routes

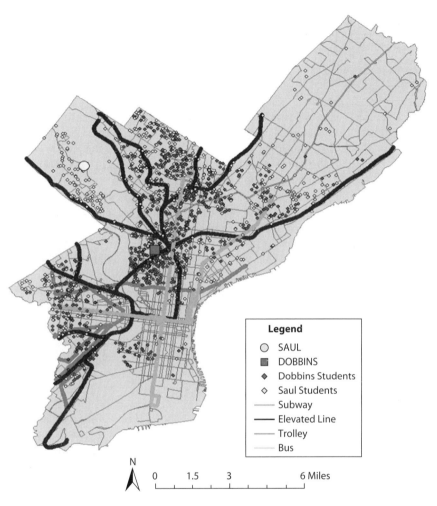

Source: Krieger (2010).

created in Figure 8.7 where Krieger (2010) plotted the location of students attending one of two schools (Saul or Dobbins), along with the location of major public transportation routes. This map can be used to examine the relationship between student home location, transit lines, and school attendance to see if greater access to public transportation influenced student attendance rates.

These are some examples showing how GIS data visualization can be used for needs assessment, tracking program implementation, and understanding some of the underlying reasons affecting program fidelity. Evaluators interested in incorporating GIS into their practice should think about

NEW DIRECTIONS FOR EVALUATION • DOI: 10.1002/ev

the added value that a geographic representation can have on understanding the program's fidelity. The best way to approach this process is through the creation of simpler maps using Google Maps (or equivalent) to depict program implementation and add program information. This would provide the evaluator with an initial sense of how geography can affect programs, before creating more advanced GIS maps.

GIS and Program Outcomes

GIS also offers evaluators the ability to examine program outcomes and how they are spread across a particular region or geographic area visually. Such images can be complex or simple, depending on the needs of the evaluation, availability of resources, and the training of the evaluator. The more complex maps can be created and tailored to show a myriad of variables and outcomes and to analyze how outcomes were affected by environmental factors. For example, in 2006 the Los Angeles Police Department (LAPD) instituted a policy called Safer Cities that resulted in the strict enforcement of minor offenses in downtown Los Angeles. This policy aimed to reduce the homeless population in the skid row area with a focus on enforcement rather than prevention. The LAPD contracted with Cartifact (2007) to map out the impact of this policy once it was implemented. Cartifact created a series of maps that tracked the distribution of homeless individuals across downtown LA (Figure 8.8). These maps showed change over time from November 2006 to June 2007 and dramatically illustrated the effect of the Safer Cities policy in reducing the number of homeless in the target area. These maps also showed where additional resources were needed and the LAPD used the maps as a communication tool with the public. These types of analysis require more sophisticated GIS and statistical expertise, but they can provide important insights about program performance across time.

Simpler maps can also be created with the use of Google Maps or Bing Maps to illustrate program outcomes for each site. An evaluator can easily create these maps by using the drag-and-drop method to identify the location of each program site. Once this process is completed, data can be color coded to denote program performance on a particular outcome. Program sites that are achieving their goals could be colored light gray, average performance programs can be darker gray, and low-performing programs can be represented by very dark gray icons (Figure 8.9). Additional information could be included to describe how each program site is performing. Such a simple map can help the evaluator and program staff visualize how programs are performing across a wide geographic region, and it may lead to insights about how each location is performing within its local environment.

Maps can also be used to document the experiences of program participants. Google Maps allows users to upload pictures that are connected to a particular location and to provide descriptions along with each photo.

Figure 8.8. An Example of a Map Showing Change Over Time

Source: www.cartifact.com

Figure 8.9. An Example of a Map Showing Program Locations and Outcomes

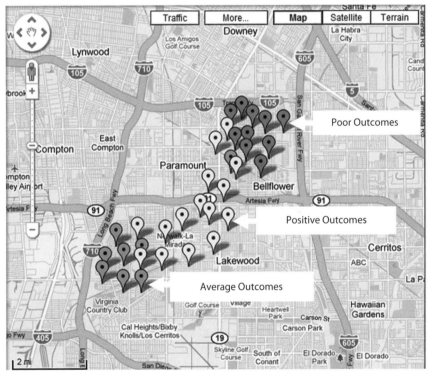

Source: www.maps.google.com

This feature was used in an evaluation of a college prep program, where students visited multiple college campuses. Students were asked to document their experiences by taking pictures of the most interesting/inspiring thing that they saw (Figure 8.10) and to provide a brief paragraph about what they learned and experienced during the visit. I used this information

Figure 8.10. A Map That Shows Pictures and Experiences of Students Visiting College Campuses

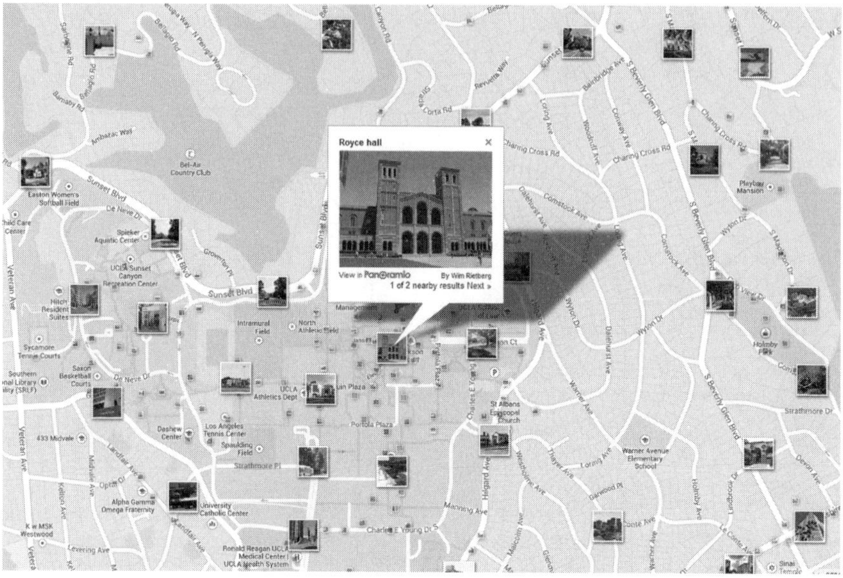

Source: www.maps.google.com

to create an "experience map" that documented the lessons learned during each campus visit. This map helped the evaluation team illustrate the knowledge gained from visits in an interactive method that used multimedia and geography to describe program outcomes. This map was well received by program staff and was later adopted as a communication tool to recruit future participants to the program.

GIS Limitations

The previous examples and discussions of GIS were meant to offer readers a wide perspective on what GIS-created maps can look like and how they can be used during the evaluation process. The goal was to show the unique contribution of maps beyond what a traditional bar chart or data table can offer. These contributions include the ability to take contextual features into account when trying to interpret program processes and outcomes and identify geographically related needs and gaps in resources. However, these unique contributions also come at a cost that requires the evaluator to be more purposeful and careful about making inferences from the visual patterns produced by GIS maps. For example, at a descriptive level, Figure 8.11 implied that Florida counties that voted for President Bush in 2000

Figure 8.11. An Example of Erroneous Causal Inference From a Map

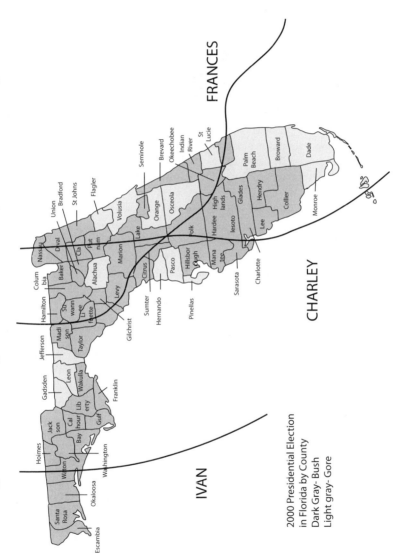

FRANCES

CHARLEY

IVAN

2000 Presidential Election
in Florida by County
Dark Gray- Bush
Light gray- Gore

were struck by multiple hurricanes as they crossed through Florida. Although this map was designed to be politically humorous, it shows how easily we can make inferential assumptions about map data and patterns.

A similar cautionary tale can be found in the first example offered in the chapter, where Figure 8.1 strongly implied an almost perfect correlation between the location of tobacco billboards and low-SES neighborhoods. The authors (Luke et al., 2000) noted that the relationship represented by Figure 8.1 was strongly influenced by the location of major freeways that tended to have many billboards and also tended to cross most low-SES communities. This example shows that users of GIS should be intimately familiar with the communities they are mapping or possess multiple sources of data to represent various community and geographic character-istics adequately before making causal inferences about the patterns found in the maps. This process is similar to disproving the counterfactual (Shad-ish, Cook, & Campbell, 2001) to identify the causal relationship between variables. GIS offers us the opportunity to account for other potential causes for program performance; however, the evaluator should proceed with care before jumping to conclusions too soon.

The other major limitation to GIS is the level of training needed to con-duct more complex analyses. I have attempted to show a range of GIS maps that were created with a variety of tools, including ArcGIS, Google Maps, Many-Eyes.com, and custom-built software solutions. The more accessible software can create simpler descriptive maps and as the complexity and ana-lytical needs increase, then the cost of the software and the training needed also increases. However, GIS-type software is becoming more common and integrated across different websites and tools, and I believe that this trend will continue in the future. One clear example is the introduction of basic GIS map-ping software into the new Microsoft Excel 365. Users can download an appli-cation into Excel (called Bing Maps for Office) and create tables with geographic information and use that table to generate a GIS-like map (Figure 8.12). This very recent development signals the mainstreaming of GIS into commonly used software and indicates that this visualization approach is here to stay.

Final Thoughts

I would like to end this chapter with a very early GIS map that was created by John Snow in 1854 (Figure 8.13), where Dr. Snow used a map to docu-ment the location of cholera deaths during a city-wide cholera epidemic (each dot represents a death).

After creating the map by hand and using his intimate knowledge of London, he noticed that most of the deaths were within walking distance of a particular water pump (marked by a circle) and that other water pumps in the area (marked by triangles) appeared to lack this concentration of fatalities. He concluded that the cholera epidemic was linked to a contaminated water pump and removed its handle. Once this was done the cholera epidemic

Figure 8.12. An Image of the New Application (Bing Maps for Office) That Allows for Basic GIS Mapping in Excel

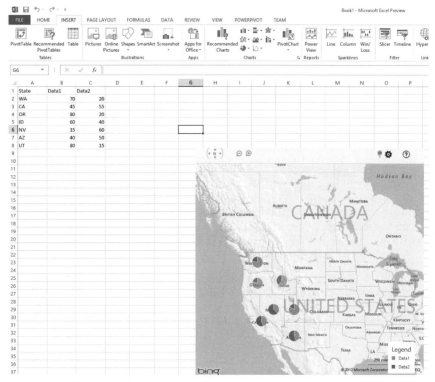

Source: http://office.microsoft.com/en-us/store/bing-maps-WA102957661.aspx

Figure 8.13. John Snow's Map of Cholera Deaths and the Location of a Contaminated Water Pump

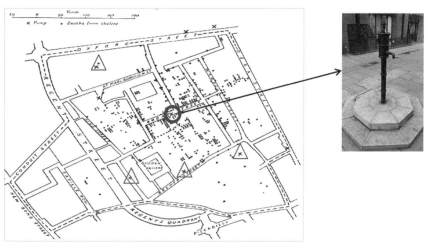

Source: http://en.wikipedia.org/wiki/John_Snow (physician)

ended and many lives were saved. This example shows the inferential power that can be gained when data, geography, intimate contextual understanding, and visualization are combined to understand a phenomenon. This power may not always save lives, as was dramatically illustrated with the Snow map, but it can help us better understand the impact of the programs and policies that we frequently evaluate and hopefully lead to improved outcomes and ultimately a higher quality of life for those being served.

References

Azzam, T., & Robinson, D. (2013). GIS in evaluation utilizing the power of geographic information systems to represent evaluation data. *American Journal of Evaluation, 34*(2), 207–224.

Cartifact. (2007). *Homeless population map: Downtown Los Angeles.* Retrieved from http://homeless.cartifact.com/webmaps/homeless/

Chang, K. (2007). *Introduction to geographic information systems* (4th ed.). Columbus, OH: McGraw-Hill.

Goodchild, M. F., & Janelle, D. G. (2004). Thinking spatially in the social sciences. In M. F. Goodchild & D. G. Janelle (Eds.), *Spatially integrated social science* (pp. 3–22). New York, NY: Oxford University Press.

Krieger, T. (2010). *A GIS-based method to study the effect of distance on student attendance rates.* Paper presented at ESRI's Mid-Atlantic User Group Conference, Philadelphia, PA. Retrieved from http://proceedings.esri.com/library/userconf/mug10/papers/gis_based_method_study_effect_distance_student_attendance_rates.pdf

Luke, D., Esmundo, E., & Bloom, Y. (2000). Smoke signs: Patterns of tobacco billboard advertising in a metropolitan region. *Tobacco Control, 9*(1), 16–23.

Renger, R., Cimetta, A., Pettrgrove, S., & Rogan, S. (2002). Geographic information systems (GIS) as an evaluation tool. *American Journal of Evaluation, 23*(4), 469–479.

Shadish, W. R., Cook, T. D., & Campbell, D. T. (2001). *Experimental and quasi-experimental designs for generalized causal inference.* Boston, MA: Houghton-Mifflin.

TAREK AZZAM is an assistant professor at Claremont Graduate University, and associate director of the Claremont Evaluation Center.

INDEX